To Traci

LIVING
PROOF

Carolyn Jones 1999

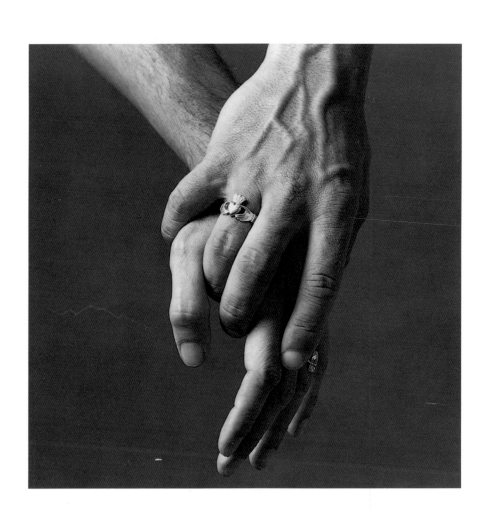

LIVING PROOF

COURAGE IN THE FACE OF AIDS

PHOTOGRAPHS BY
CAROLYN JONES

CONCEPT BY
GEORGE DeSIPIO, JR.

FOREWORD BY
IAN McKELLEN

INTRODUCTION BY
MICHAEL LIBERATORE

ABBEVILLE PRESS PUBLISHERS
NEW YORK   LONDON   PARIS

NOTE: In the captions, names in capital letters indicate which
sitters are HIV-positive.

Front cover: **RICHARD MAGPIONG**

I have always enjoyed singing duets more than arias or solos, because I like the
dynamic of collaborating, of cooperating, of trying to breathe in sync and sing
harmony with another performer. I think this can be a very beneficial way of
looking at a relationship with a doctor while dealing with AIDS. What a sense
of self-empowerment would ensue if that relationship were a true collaboration!
It would be so much better than feeling like a victim and presenting one's
disease to a health-care worker saying, "Here, you cure me."

Back cover: **GEORGE DeSIPIO, JR., and Michael Liberatore**

PROJECT EDITOR: Laura Straus
TEXT EDITOR: Alice Gray
DESIGNER: Patricia Fabricant
PRODUCTION EDITOR: Abigail Asher
PRODUCTION MANAGER: Simone René

Library of Congress Cataloging-in-Publication Data
Jones, Carolyn.
Living Proof : courage in the face of AIDS / photographs by Carolyn
Jones ; foreword by Ian McKellen ; introduction by Michael Liberatore.
p.   cm.
ISBN 1-55859-713-1
1. AIDS (Disease)—Patients—Pictorial works.   I. Title.
RC607.A26J657   1994
362.1'969792'00222—dc20   93—44062
                                                    CIP

THIS BOOK WAS MADE POSSIBLE
WITH A GENEROUS GRANT FROM THE
HOWARD GILMAN FOUNDATION

AND THE *LIVING PROOF* COMMITTEE:

GEORGE DeSIPIO, JR.
GEORGIA GOODROW
WILL GUILLIAMS
DAVID KLEINBERG
MICHAEL LIBERATORE
BILLY O'CONNOR
JACK ROSENBERG
JOHN WESSEL

F O R E W O R D

by Ian McKellen

L ooking at this collection of photographs for the first time, you ask yourself, "What do these people have in common?" At first glance, the answer might seem trivial. These ordinary-looking people—so like our friends and acquaintances—reveal few hints of home, income, or lifestyle. Maybe they just share a birthday or a passion for ice cream. Have they, perhaps, all met the president or the Pope or each other? *That* might be it: they could all live in the same town. Would anyone ever have guessed that these people share a virus? Take a second look, then a third.

Each of them was invited to a completely bare studio, where there were no distractions in the background. In the photographs, they clearly wear their own clothes, exhibiting a relaxation that those black-and-white ads for jeans never quite achieve. These are not models, they are not on display. They do, however, all seem to want to be photographed. No doubt Carolyn Jones put them at ease. But they haven't just been captured by her loving camera; they have captivated her lens. Their charisma has put them in control. That is what vitally connects them—not just the shared virus but a self-confidence about the disease and about life; they communicate a tremendous sense of exhilaration. These are not ordinary people after all.

Before HIV/AIDS had an official name, all we heard were confusing rumors. The virus was called the "gay cancer"; it came from monkeys, from Africans, from Haitians; it had escaped from a madman's laboratory. None of it seemed real enough to be our personal concern. By the time the media admitted that it was the story of the century, we were being encouraged to think that the disease was a punishment and that it had, somehow, been created by its carriers. That can be true of any plague, if we identify the carrier as ignorance and poverty and a belief that nothing can be done.

At the same time we read about "innocent victims": hemophiliacs infected by "poisoned" blood transfusions, babies infected by drug-addicted mothers. But as HIV/AIDS spread—especially throughout major metropolitan areas—more and more of us had friends who got sick, and famous people died. AIDS became a challenge. Money was raised for research, support groups were formed to provide care, and lobbies were created to persuade. Everyone, whether HIV positive or negative, had a story to tell. What moves me most about Carolyn Jones's portraits is that they tell no detailed stories, but they reveal everything about her subjects' inner lives. Miraculously, she has photographed people's souls.

Nationalism flares up, famine rages, and the ozone layer burns. Yet, when history eventually passes judgment on our apocalyptic age, surely the decisive question will be: "What did they do about AIDS?" What did the United Nations do, across the world? What did the politicians do, nationally and locally? And the churches and commerce and the media? What did any of us do?

Even now, during the second decade of the pandemic, it's clear that too many of us have done too little. But blame and anger are only part of the story. The whole truth of AIDS can't be found in the inertia of government, in the exaggerations of the media, or in the bigots' lies. AIDS has unleashed great power in individuals and in groups—among people who have learned how to care and counsel, who have organized their consciences.

At the heart of the matter are the people who know the most about living with this disease—the people in this book. The truth about HIV/AIDS shines from their faces, bodies, hands, feet, and smiles, which have captivated the camera for our enlightenment.

London, 1993

INTRODUCTION

Living Proof was born in November 1991, when I sat by George DeSipio's bedside in New York Hospital. We were lovers, and he was recuperating from his first bout of pneumocystis (AIDS-related pneumonia). He was infuriated by the lack of positive imagery in the media regarding people with AIDS. George felt that without a life-affirming view of how individuals deal with this illness, many people with AIDS might give up hope for ever living a full life. Swearing that if he recovered he would find a way to present a constructive portrait of what living—really living—with AIDS was all about, George outlined the concept that became our project. We decided to organize an exhibition that would illustrate that an AIDS diagnosis is not an immediate death sentence.

I am an art director, so my first duty was to find a photographer who would share our vision and capture our message on film. We needed an artist who was not only technically superb, but who also had the heart and soul to create images that would both comfort and motivate those who were desperate for a ray of hope. Instantly, I thought of Carolyn Jones. I had worked with Carolyn for years, and I believe she is the best portrait photographer around. And I love her. Her interest in her subjects is all-consuming, and her manner is wonderfully reassuring; many a friendship has been formed in her studio. I confess I was overwhelmed with guilt about asking Carolyn to tackle a project of such proportion, yet when I presented the idea to her, she answered yes without a moment's hesitation.

We agreed that our best approach would be to do a series of large-format black-and-white portraits of everyday people, people who were outstanding only in their commitment to making every minute count, in refusing to surrender to AIDS. Simultaneously, Carolyn and I decided to ask our sitters to pose with whomever or whatever kept them going strong. And so our odyssey began. We canvassed New York City for willing subjects, and in April 1992, we began to shoot. Carolyn photographed and interviewed each candidate and relayed their stories to both George and me. As she worked, something beautiful began to bloom— not just the fruit of our efforts, but an attitude of caring that enveloped everyone who became involved. Photo assistants, caterers, film processors, hair and makeup artists all volunteered long hours; media people gave us exposure with very little coercing; and people with AIDS came forward to be photographed in numbers far greater than we had ever imagined. The parade of beloved friends, family, and cherished objects that were brought to the studio was truly touching, and the resulting images told stories of passion, wisdom, and tenacity. When it came time to title our efforts, I couldn't think of anything more appropriate than *Living Proof,* because that is what this project provides: proof that people with AIDS are vital and spirited individuals courageously facing an overwhelming adversary. And proof that people have not forgotten how to care.

Throughout the next two years, we never lost faith in our mission or in its original intent. Sadly, some of our subjects are no longer with us, among them George DeSipio, Jr., whose vision launched this project and whose optimism and dignity are expressed on these pages. Their strength continues to inspire and educate others. Jason Snipe, a student at P.S. 234 in New York City, saw our first gallery presentation at the World Trade Center on World AIDS Day in 1992. His teacher had brought his sixth-grade class, and she asked them to write to Carolyn about *Living Proof.* "I liked your portraits because they showed that people with AIDS are as normal and regular as anyone else. If somebody hadn't told me that these people had AIDS I wouldn't have known. They seemed so happy. I wish them the best, and thank you for showing people that they are as normal as us."

—**MICHAEL LIBERATORE,** New York City, 1993

HENRY NICOLS

I decided to make the disclosure of my HIV status part of
my Eagle Scout project. I started an AIDS education program
in my school and my community, and in the process, told everyone I had AIDS. People often ask me what my plans are, because,
I think, they want to know if somebody with AIDS has long-
term plans. I've been living with this virus for close to ten years
now, and I don't think of myself as a victim. I'm just a person
living with a virus. My long-term plans are simple:
in 2008, I'm running for President.

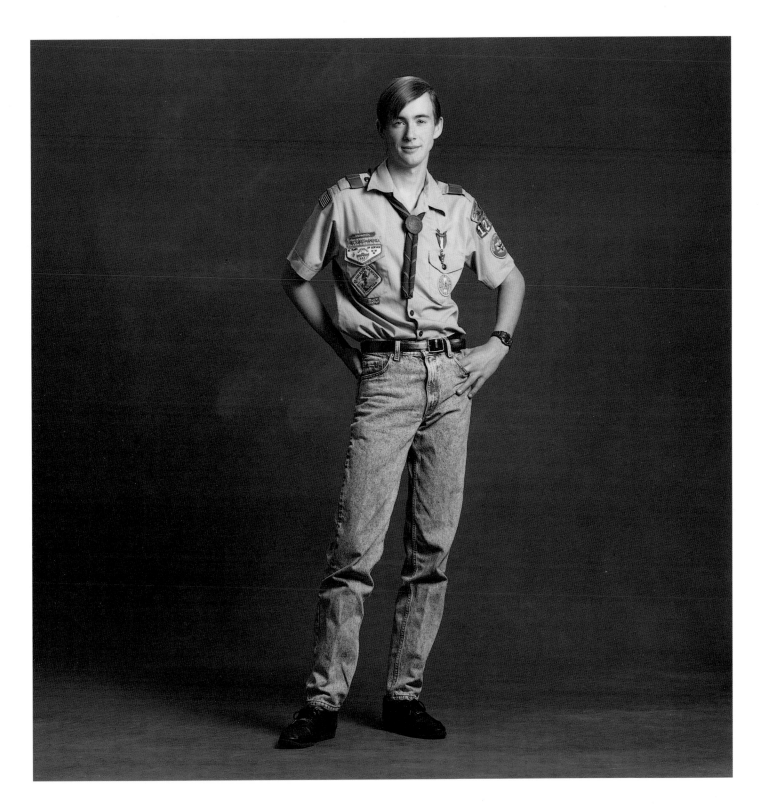

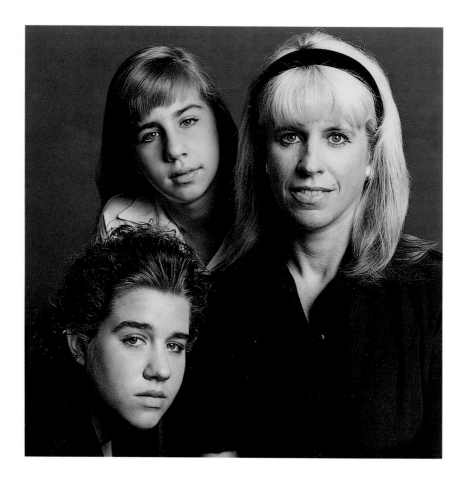

MARY HANERFELD and her daughters

I have blonde hair and blue eyes, and I feel I can send a message to middle
America: it can happen to anybody. I was in the drugstore and I heard this
woman say something about AIDS and gays, and I said, "Honey, you're looking
at it—AIDS." People are so ignorant, and their ignorance breeds fear. I'm not
fearful of death, I'm just afraid of the pain that AIDS is going to cause.

[OPPOSITE]

WILLIAM ELLSWORTH THOMPSON II
(also known as Adé Omawali)

Once I was able to fully accept my AIDS diagnosis, the doors of life were no
longer closed to me. Being African-American, gay, and Afro-eccentric allows
me to express my creativity within my own culture. This is my reality and I live
it to the max. It is one thing to survive, but achieving a high quality of life
with AIDS is more than an art form, it's a gift from God.

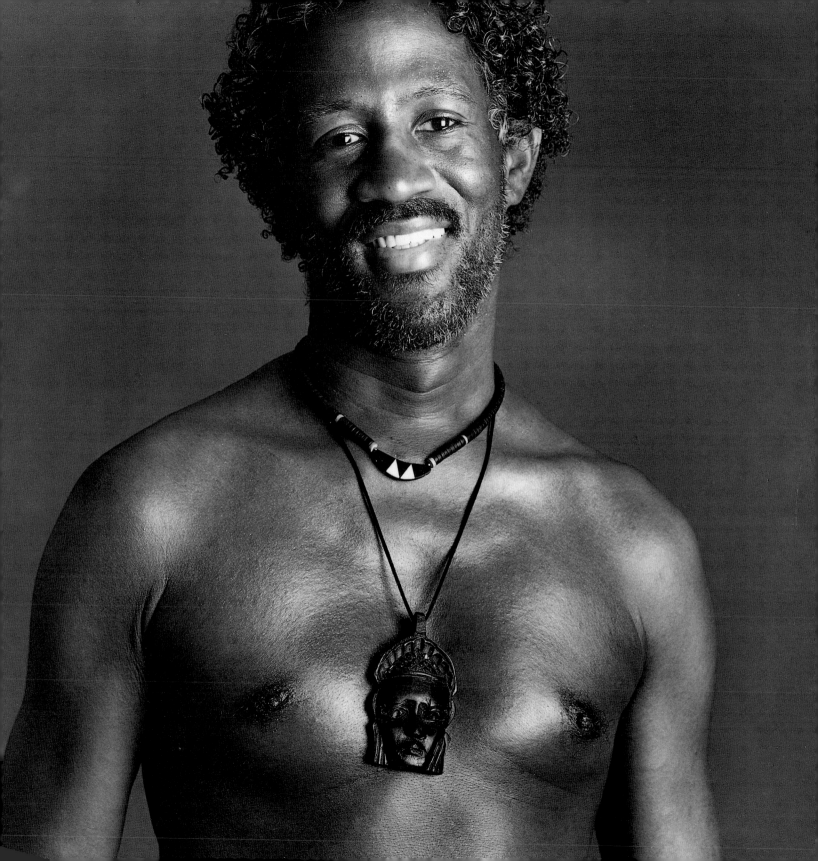

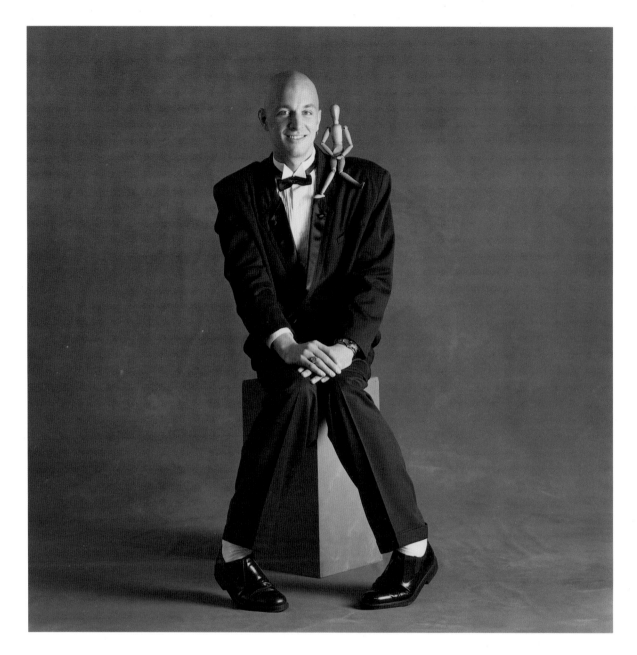

ROSS JOHNSON (1966–1993)

Testing positive was a wake-up call. Since I found out, I've learned how to live. And maybe I've found my life's work—teaching people not to be afraid of who they are or of this epidemic. AIDS is a social disease, and I don't just mean the virus in people's bodies or how it is transmitted, but how society deals with it. It's not like getting the measles or breaking a leg, when all of your neighbors show up at your door with lasagna. People shun you; they are desperately afraid. And of what? It's just Ross Johnson, the boy next door.

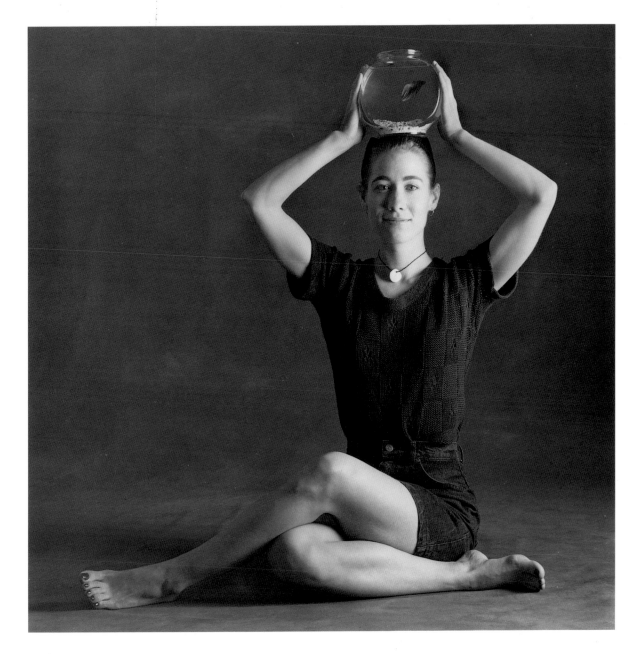

VANESSA CLARK

A single fish in a bowl is a small piece of life in its own contained world. It reminds me of how
small the human race is in the grand scheme of things. There is a certain sadness to that,
but there is a greatness to it all.

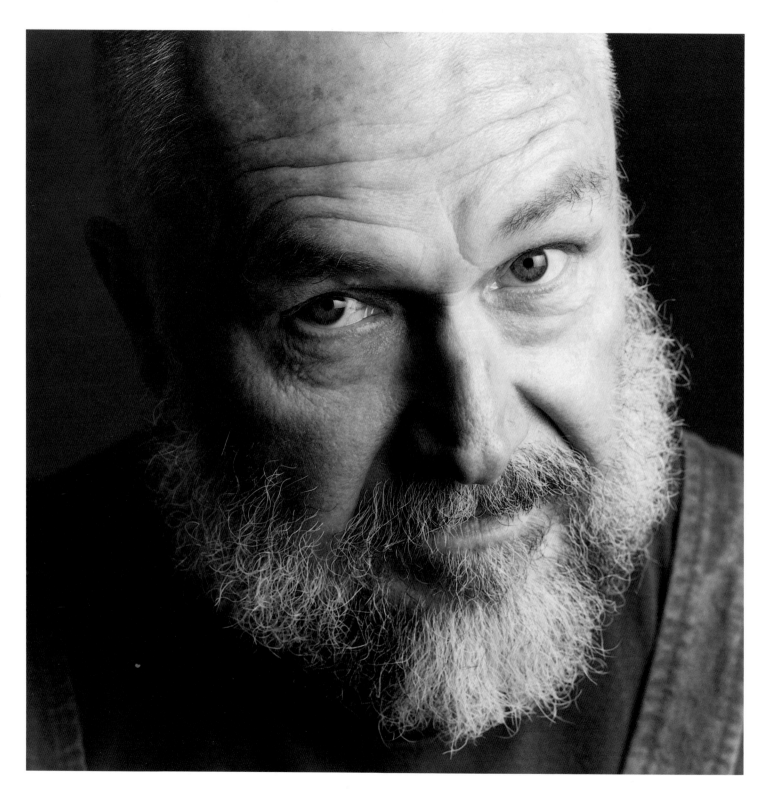

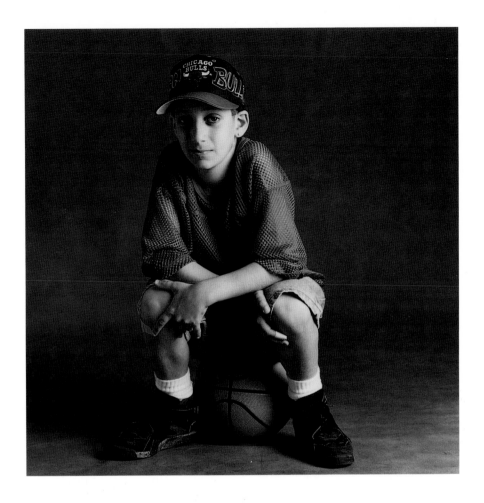

JOEY DiPAOLO

If you know someone with AIDS, don't be afraid, be a friend.

[OPPOSITE]

CALVIN YEOMANS

I knew when I chose to remain sexually active during a sexually transmittable plague that there was a chance I would be exposed to the virus that causes AIDS. But having fought all my adult life for sexual and human liberation, I had no choice but to adopt the safest sex practices I could and proceed. Having glimpsed a world of unstinting love and joy, I could not turn back. Accidents happen and warriors are wounded in battle. In 1990 I became HIV positive. My first thought was of immediate death. Ha! Certainly it will claim me one day, as it will you. Meanwhile, I reach out for all the support that is available in my community for people living with HIV, and I find more love and joy, spiritual and physical, than ever before. Sex is good. It is not going away.

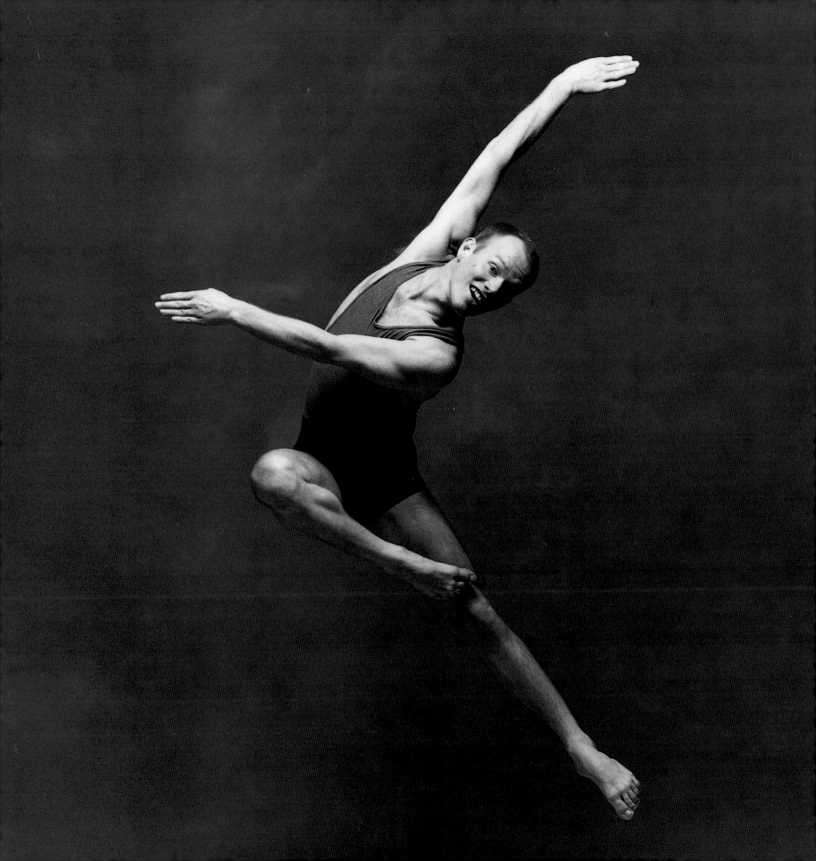

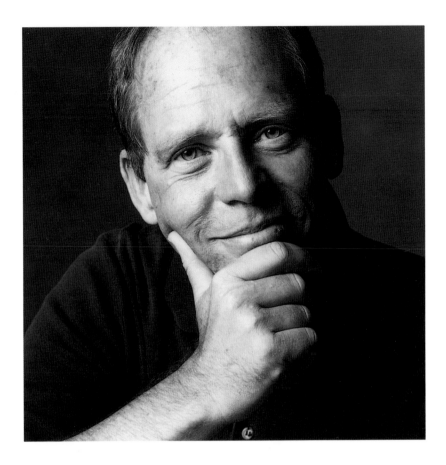

RUSS RADLEY
Director of Philanthropy, Design Industries Foundation for AIDS

Living with AIDS is an experience filled with immense irony—
the loss, hurt, sadness, and anger of it all. At the same time, you find
countless examples of boundless human will, spirit, and compassion
at their most brilliant.

[OPPOSITE]

JEFF WADLINGTON

To dance is to live. Dancing connects me to God, myself, my fellow
man, and most importantly, to life itself.

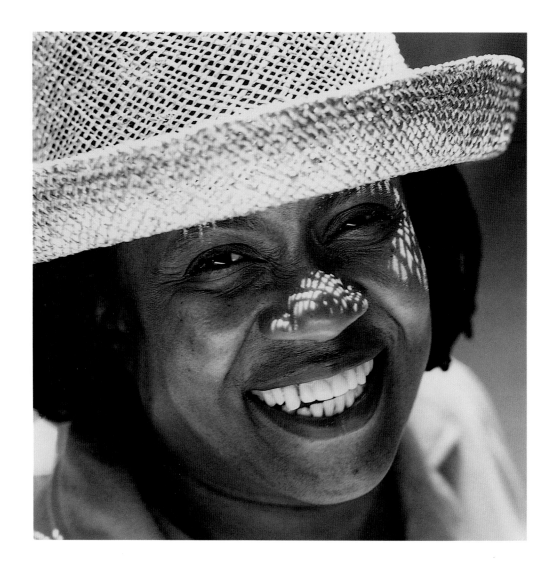

CONSTANCE TOOMER

What keeps me going is my tremendous faith and my healthy attitude toward living.
AIDS is a disease, not a disgrace.

[OPPOSITE]

ROBERT VAGELL, JR.

Hatred and ignorance are killing all that nature loves.

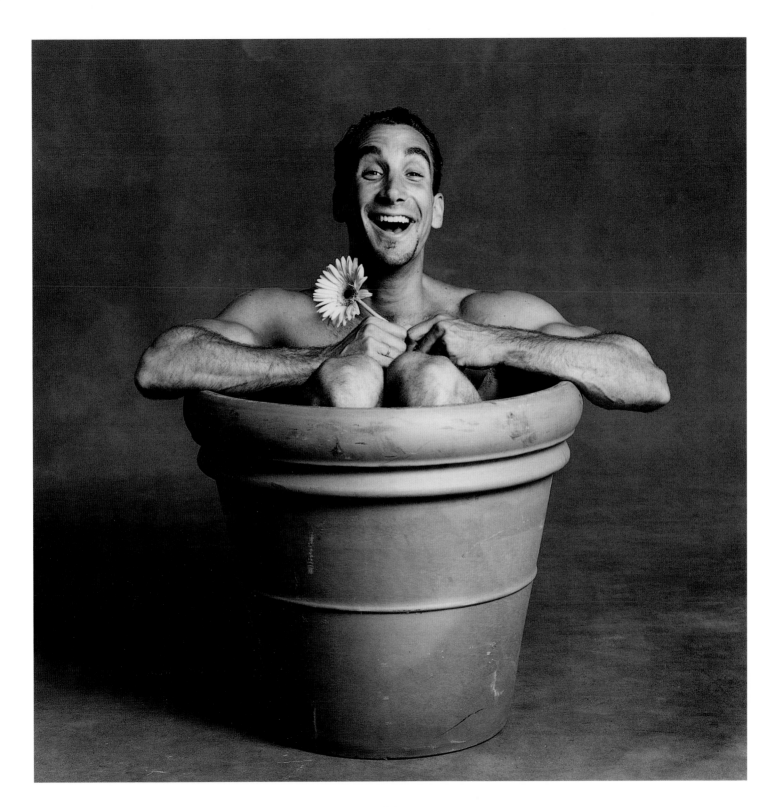

ROB HADLEY

When Carolyn Jones and George DeSipio came before a monthly G.O.A.L. (Gay Officers Action League) meeting looking for someone to photograph, I didn't feel like a hero by coming forward, I just did what I felt I had to do. Being comfortable about the disclosure of my HIV status is as important as being open about my sexuality. Both cases require taking a risk, but the results make the quality of my life, and ultimately that of those around me, so much better. I work in a conservative suburb of Chicago, and though I have heard of other cops turning their backs on their gay peers, my fellow officers have accepted me completely. The only rejection I have felt has come from gay men who want nothing to do with me when they learn I'm HIV positive. And that hurts.

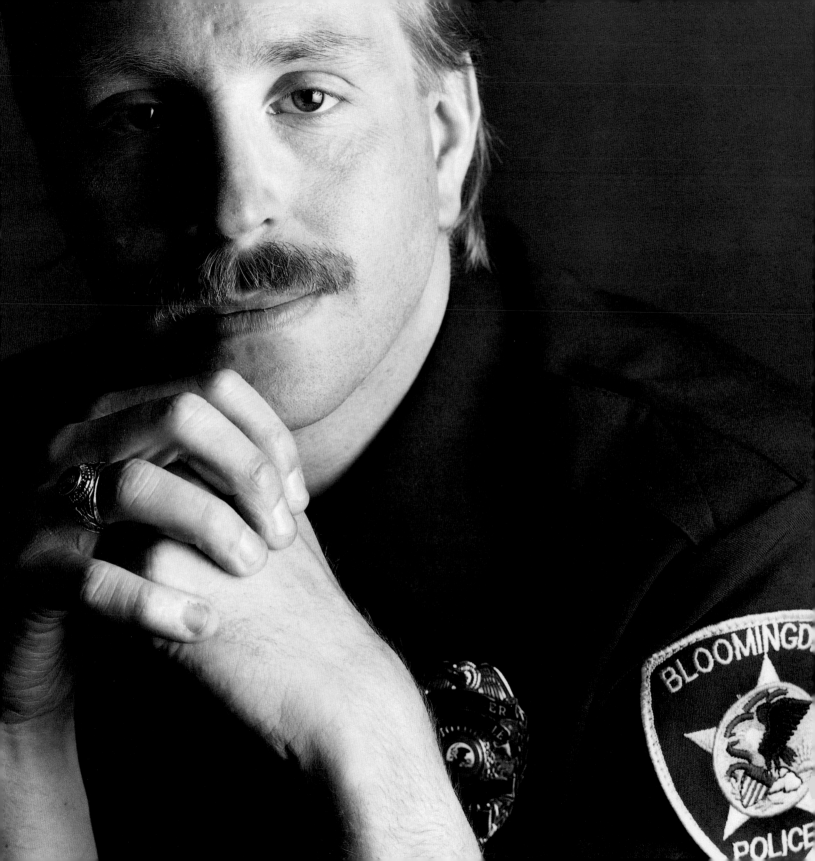

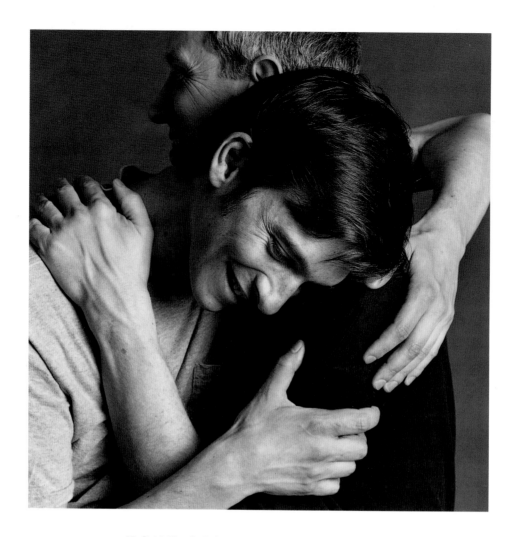

TONY GONDA (left) and friend

The last few years have been a rollercoaster of emotions, sickness, and discovery. I am one of those people who sees life as an adventure; this is simply another one. All the wise people I know, and the heroes I have read about, are just human beings. We all have our strengths and weaknesses. I've made my mistakes, some of which I've learned from, but I have lived my life; I've gotten my hands dirty. I'm proud of myself. This short story has been a damn interesting one, and it's not over yet.

[OPPOSITE]

B. W. HONEYCUTT

My hammock from the coast of North Carolina anchors me to the dreams that brought me to New York. The Polaroid photograph I hold to my heart is of the love of my life; it reminds me of the freeing possibilities of love.

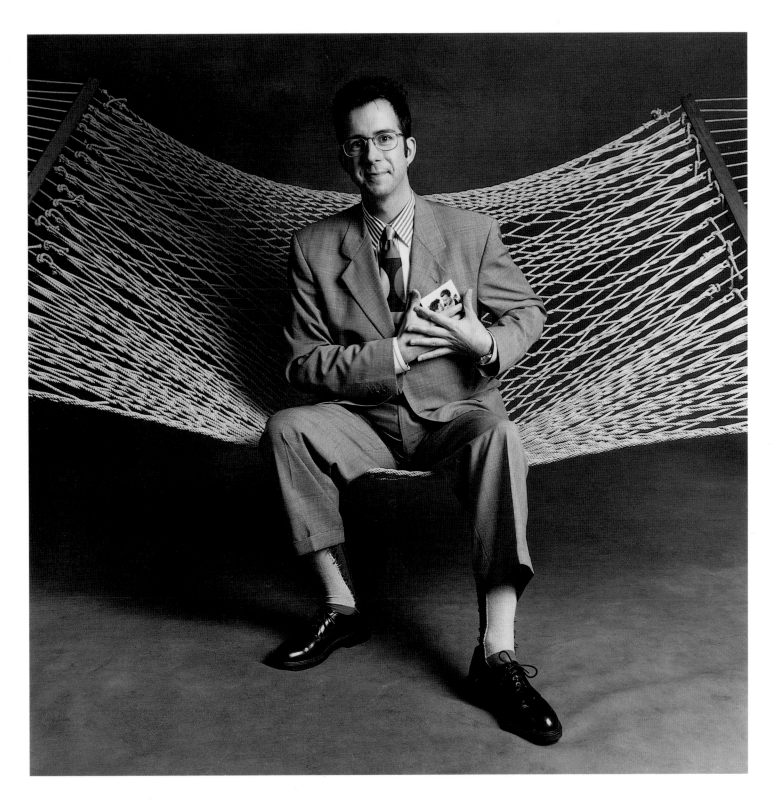

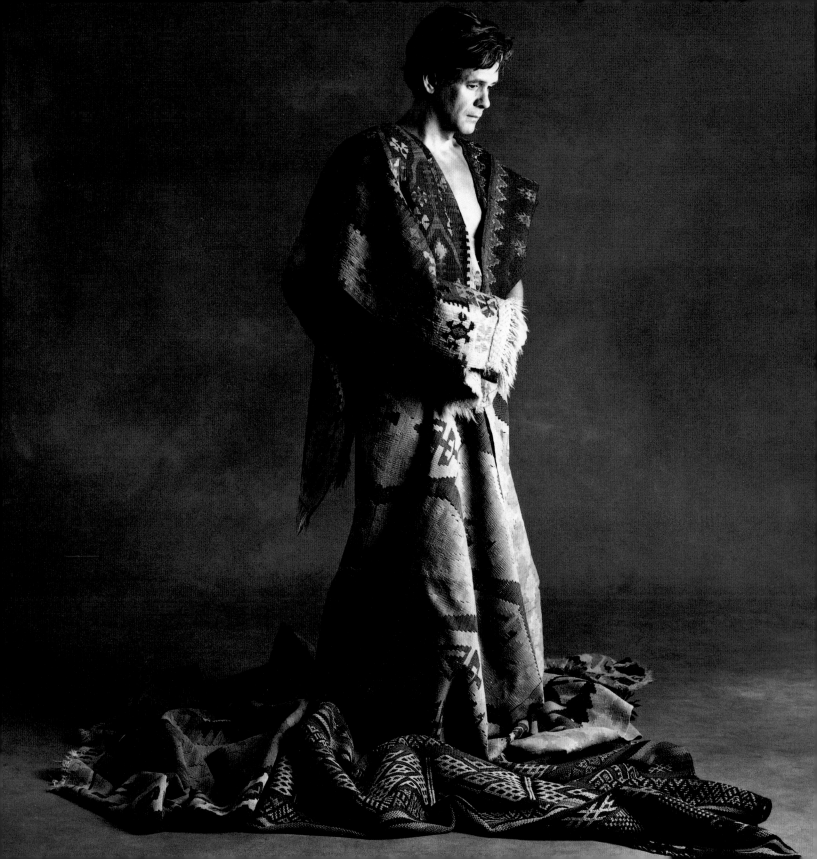

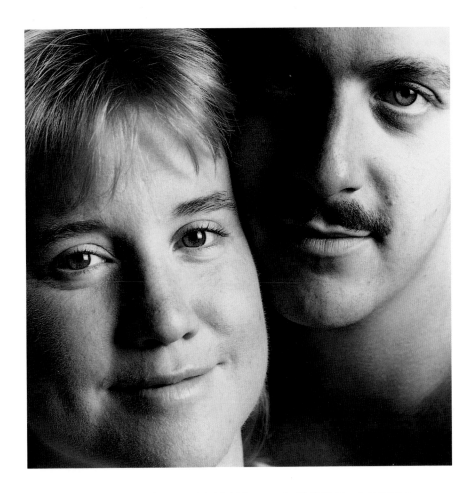

LIZ TROCHYMENKO and KURT BOYER

LIZ: Living with AIDS. I am living, not dying, from AIDS. This journey has brought many miracles, like unconditional love from my soulmate, Kurt, and the ability to forgive myself and others. I'm learning how to play again, which really is a gift. Having learned all of this has enabled me to reach out to others and truly communicate; it is a miracle and I am grateful.

KURT: If I remain teachable, HIV will continue to enlighten me. It is teaching me how to unconditionally love myself, Elizabeth, my family, all living creatures, and Mother Earth. Best of all, it motivates me to learn and grow *now*. What keeps me positive? Gratitude. Gratitude keeps me where I belong, out of the center of the universe. See you in the spirit world.

[OPPOSITE]

RAY

Wherever I go, my rugs go. Wherever they are is my home. They were the first thing I brought with me when I moved to New York. They are my passion. I began collecting rugs in 1976. Each rug has a unique story. One was a gift from a Russian aristocrat, and I feel certain it was once part of a royal palace. Another has traveled from Morocco to Australia to Spain to New York, and it will soon leave for London. It is my flying magic carpet that has been all around the world.

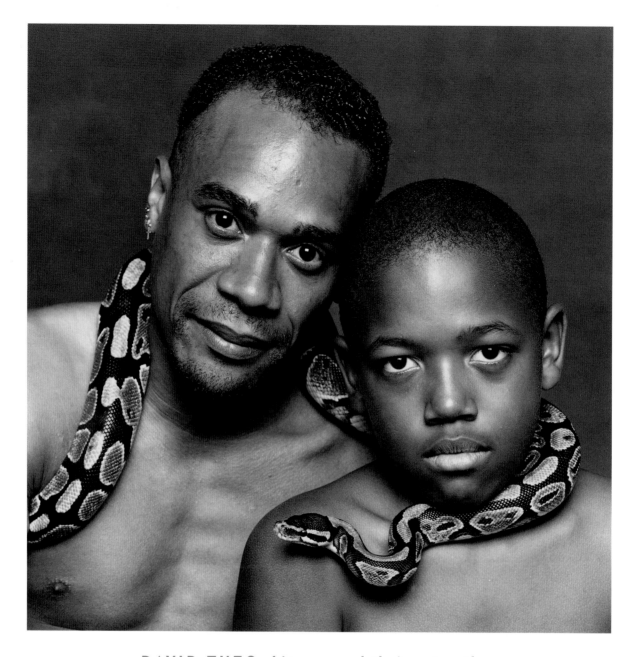

DAVID TUZO, his son, and their pet python

Being HIV positive opened my eyes to life, which I was so blind to before. I began to enjoy the simple things that people take for granted, like nature, the creatures of the Earth, and children, who carry so much love in their hearts. I'm living life over again with my nine-year-old son, and I believe that seeing my life through his eyes is healing me. I gain strength through his joy and his smile. AIDS has allowed me a second chance—a new life after the hell of drugs and alcohol that I lived before. Life is what you make it, and with my son's love, I'll live forever.

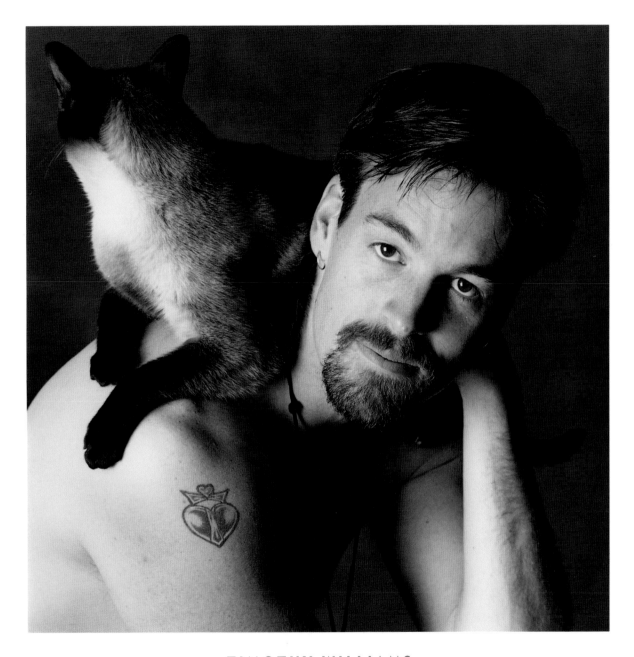

TIMOTHY WILLIAMS

In the words of Auntie Mame, "Life's a banquet." I'm enjoying every course.

ZOË LORENZ and her daughter

At fourteen, I met my biological father, who introduced me to drugs. Years later, I watched him die of AIDS, plagued not only by the disease, but by the humiliation and shame so often associated with it. I strive for a death free from shame. I wish people would look at my nine years of sobriety and not concentrate on the mistakes I made in the past. I have a beautiful four-year-old daughter who has beat the odds and remains HIV negative. People ask me, "How can you kiss her?" They actually believe you can transmit HIV through a kiss. They don't see the tragedy of this child losing her mommy. So many people have the attitude that I should go off and die somewhere alone. I'm tired of defending myself. I don't need to be proud that I have AIDS, but I won't be ashamed that I do. I don't want to feel that I have to tell people I've got cancer or some other acceptable disease.

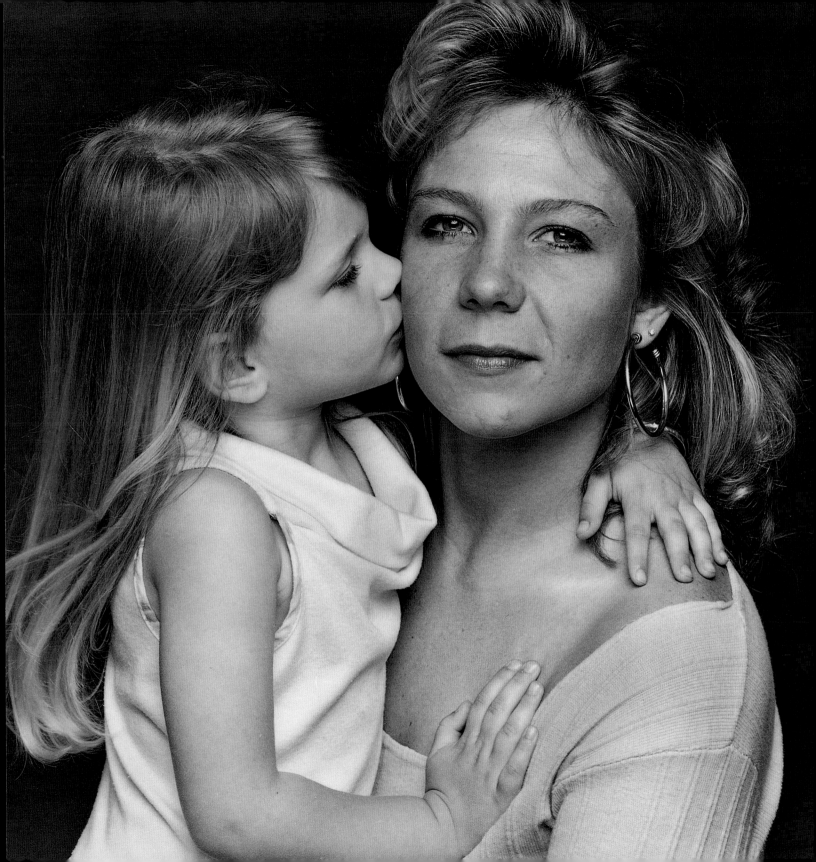

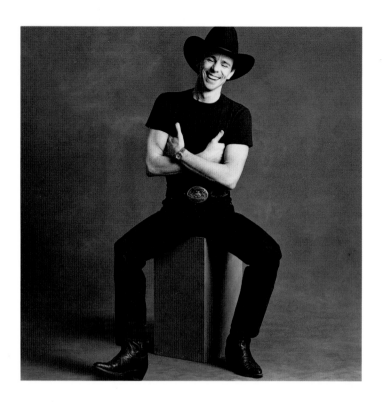

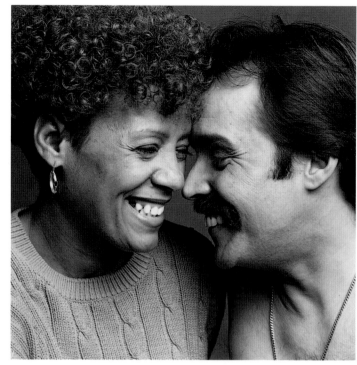

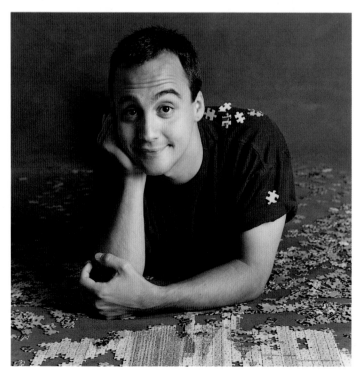

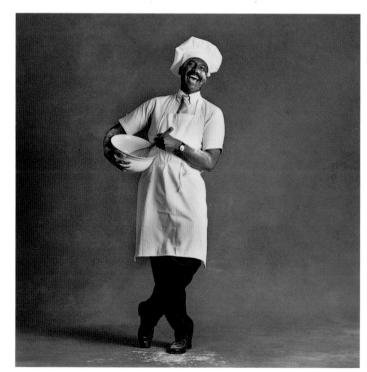

DAVID HANEY (1958–1993)

I definitely had an it-will-never-happen-to-me attitude. But AIDS doesn't discriminate; it can choose anybody. My whole life has changed. I've grown up and grown introspective. I used to be so image-conscious; only the pretty people mattered to me. Now I know that what really matters is being alive. I put up with more than I ever thought I was capable of—pain, depression. If you had told me a year ago that this was what lay ahead, I'd have said I'd rather jump off a bridge. But here I am, still dealing with it.

MILLIE ORTEZ and CARLOS CUREBEL

Carlos and I met in an HIV support group. He was really bent out of shape about his illness. I decided that we should become friends, and after about two months, he asked me out. We were walking home from a movie, and I said, "I don't date people who smoke, Carlos." He took his pack of cigarettes and said, "Look!", and threw them out into the street. He quit smoking, although it only lasted a month. But he tried, for me, he tried. He's very sick now, and his spirits are low, but I am still here for him.

RONALD JOHNSON
New York City Coordinator for AIDS Policy

Cooking is a passion for me. It allows me to escape from the tension and stress of my sometimes insane life. I'm also attracted to the immediate, concrete results that come from cooking—knowing if I've created a master-piece or a disaster, whether I'll get smiles or a look of disdain. It's not just the joy of cooking—it's the suspense that excites me.

JEFFREY GROSSI

damaged are the cells
scattered
unable to be fit
a puzzled disease
the pieces of life
find themselves
eventually

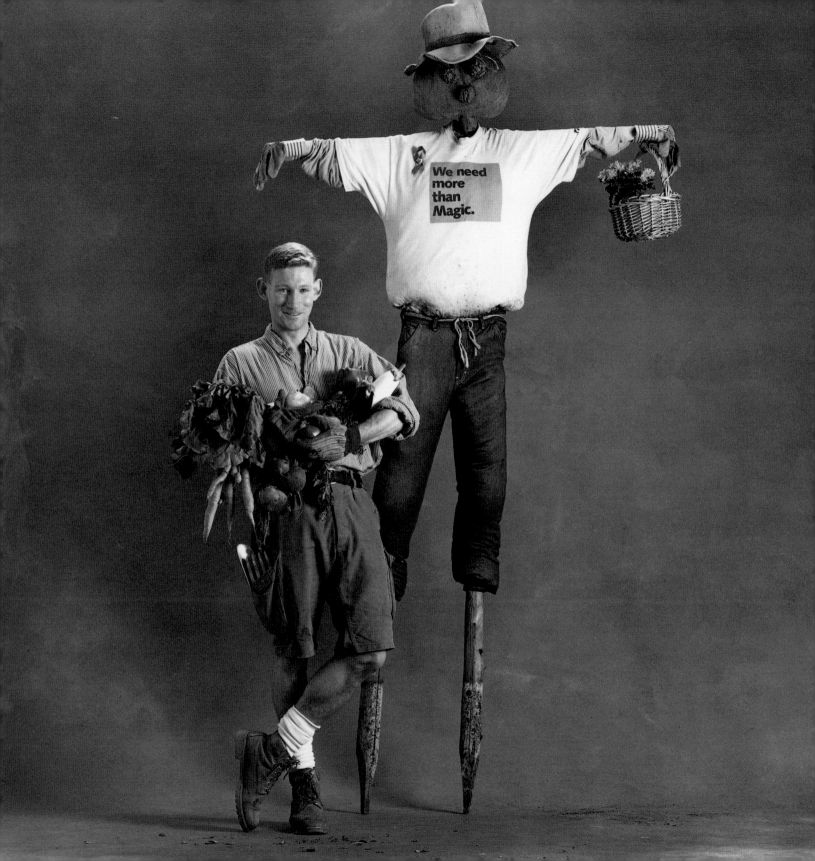

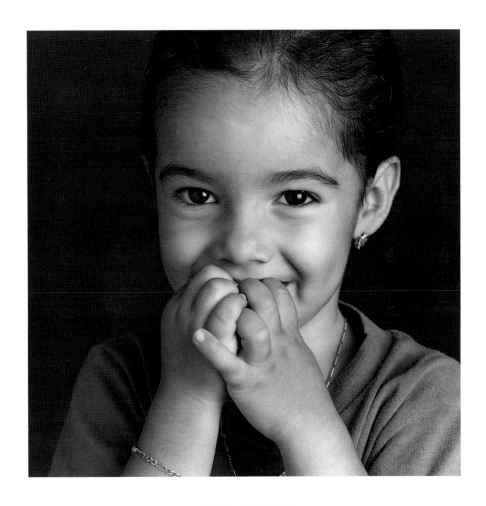

VERONICA

Veronica and her mother are both HIV positive. Veronica has no idea that
she is any different from other children.

[OPPOSITE]

JOE GUIMENTO

This is my letter to the World   Her Message is committed
That never wrote to Me—   To Hands I cannot see—
The simple News that Nature told— For love of Her—Sweet—countrymen—
With tender Majesty   Judge tenderly—of Me

—Emily Dickinson
Final Harvest, 1862

DON ADLER and his mother

My mother and I didn't always get along. We had a relationship that was not grounded in the truth. About two years ago we confronted some very tough, very personal issues and stripped away all of the lies. It was liberating to speak openly with her. We've spent the last few years building a relationship based on trust and encouragement. For the first time in my life, I know she loves me.

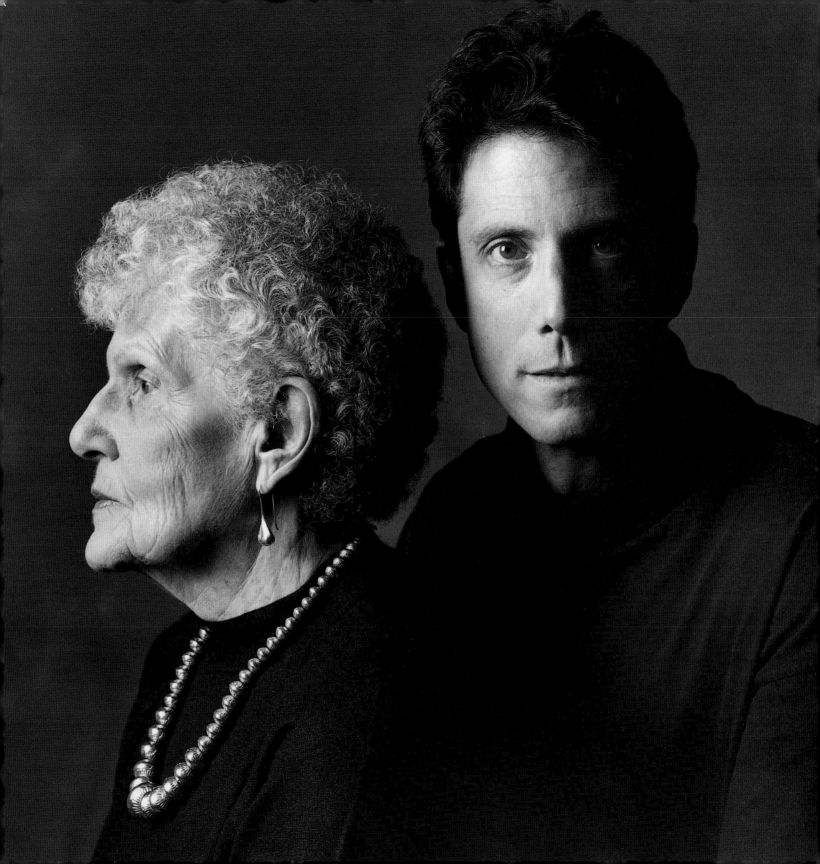

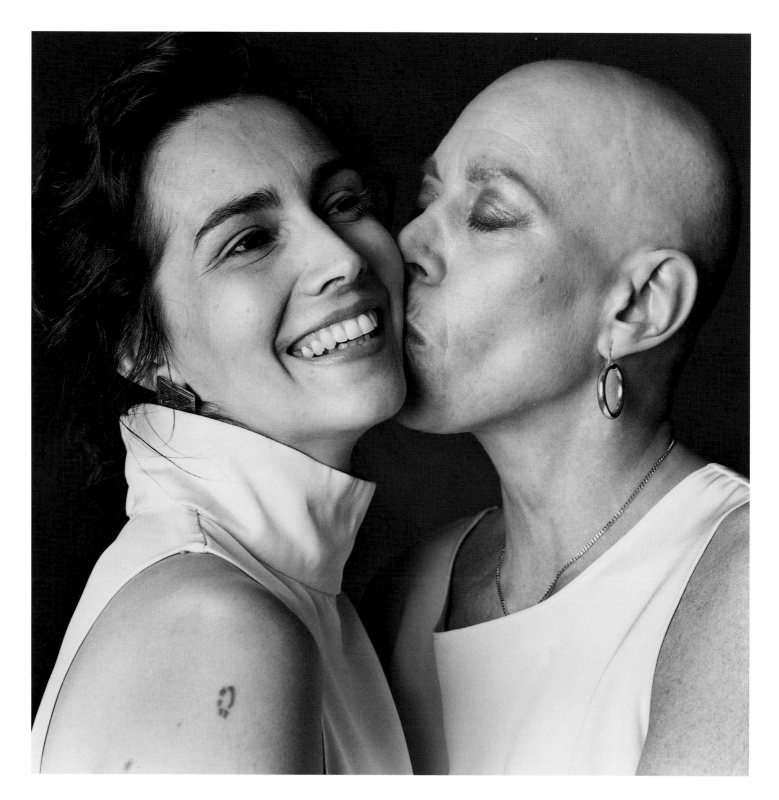

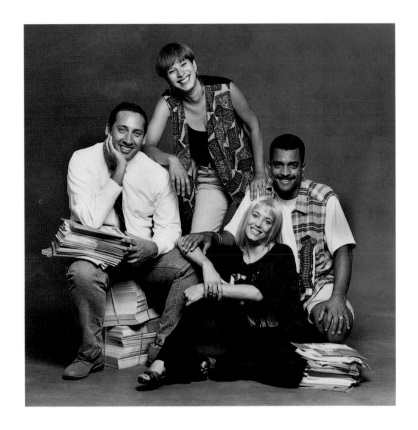

[ABOVE: CLOCKWISE FROM TOP]

MELLY'S O. VILLANUEVA, KEVIN McMASTERS, DR. CLEO ODZER, and FRANK CARBONE
of Body Positive

Body Positive provides support for people with HIV and their families, friends, and partners when they first recognize the impact of HIV on their lives.

[OPPOSITE]

PHYLLIS MARKS (right) and her partner Leila

I feel so old when I think of all the treatments I've had. But I've learned a lot. I've learned how to stand up for myself, how to accept a doctor's information and then choose whether or not I should follow his advice. It was hard to be on chemotherapy and have this picture taken. I'm not afraid of dying, but losing my hair scares me. I was someone who used to run from people who looked different or were sick. Love was just physical. Now love is community, a deep sense of sharing.

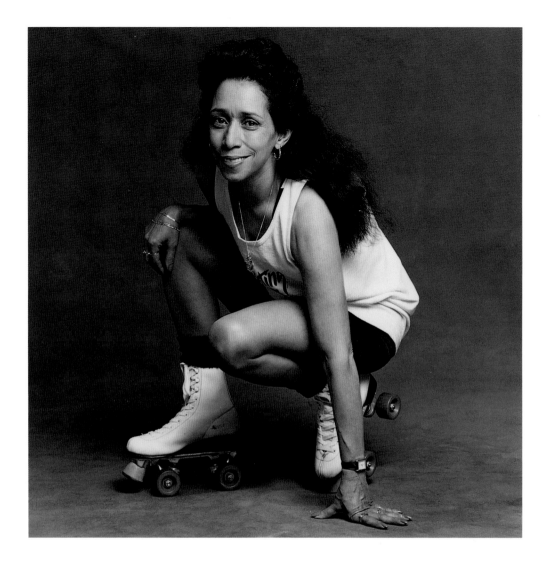

VILMA SANTIAGO, grandmother of seven

I'm a face, not a number.

[OPPOSITE]

ADRIENNE and her father

He's my best friend. He taught me to honor and love myself,
and he always puts a smile on my face.

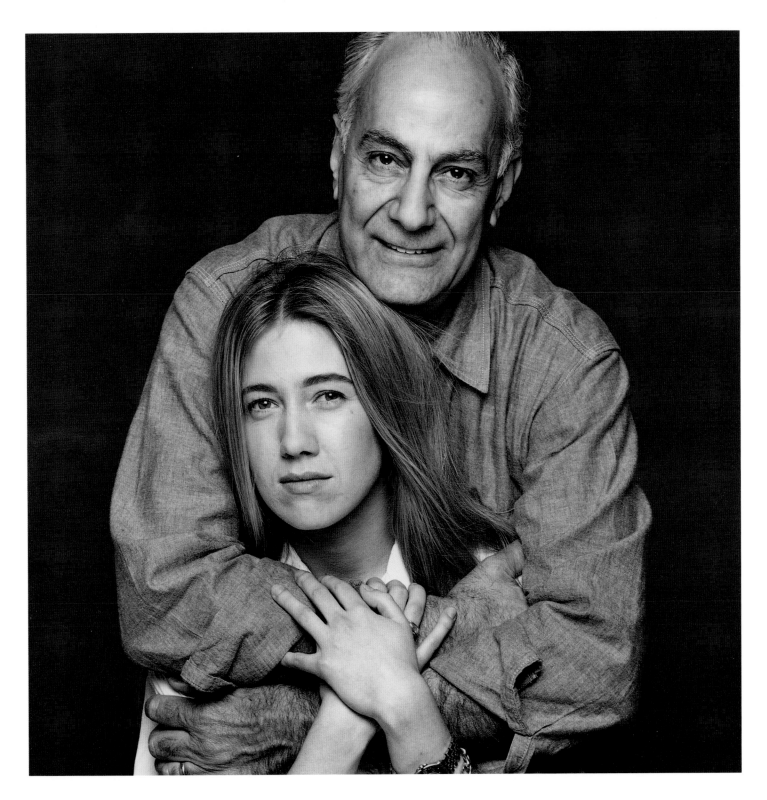

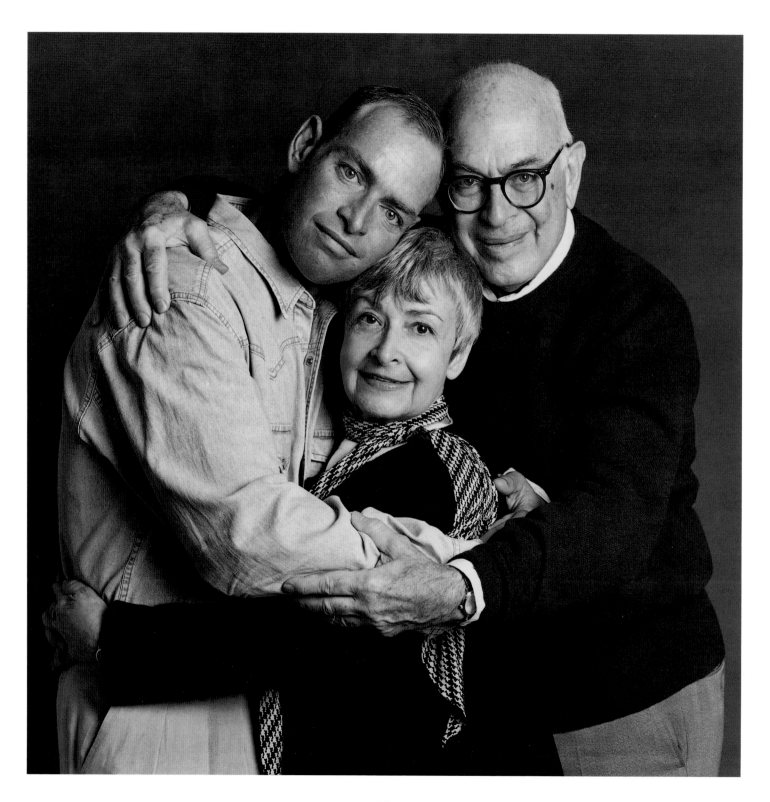

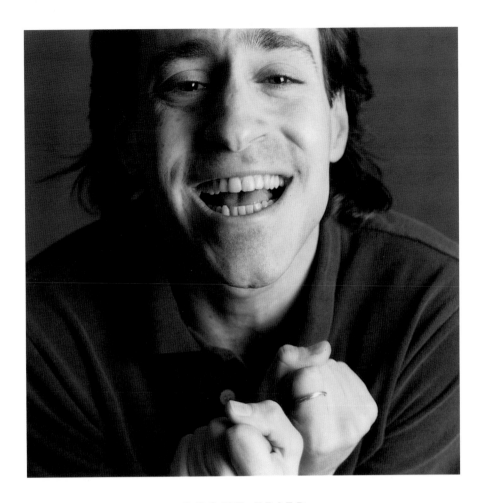

SCOTT FRIED

I was working in a law firm and I realized it was time to follow my passion,
which is singing. I'm alive!

[OPPOSITE]

GEORGE DeSIPIO, JR. (1956–1993)
and his parents

AIDS brings out the very best and the very worst in people. Some succumb
to their fears and some triumph over their illness. I've seen people really
come to terms with themselves and find happiness and peace of mind, and
I've seen people who have been defeated by it, who have pushed their
friends and family away and have died isolated and alienated. You can't deal
with this disease alone. You need to reach out to people with love. If you
reach out with love, you get love back ten-fold.

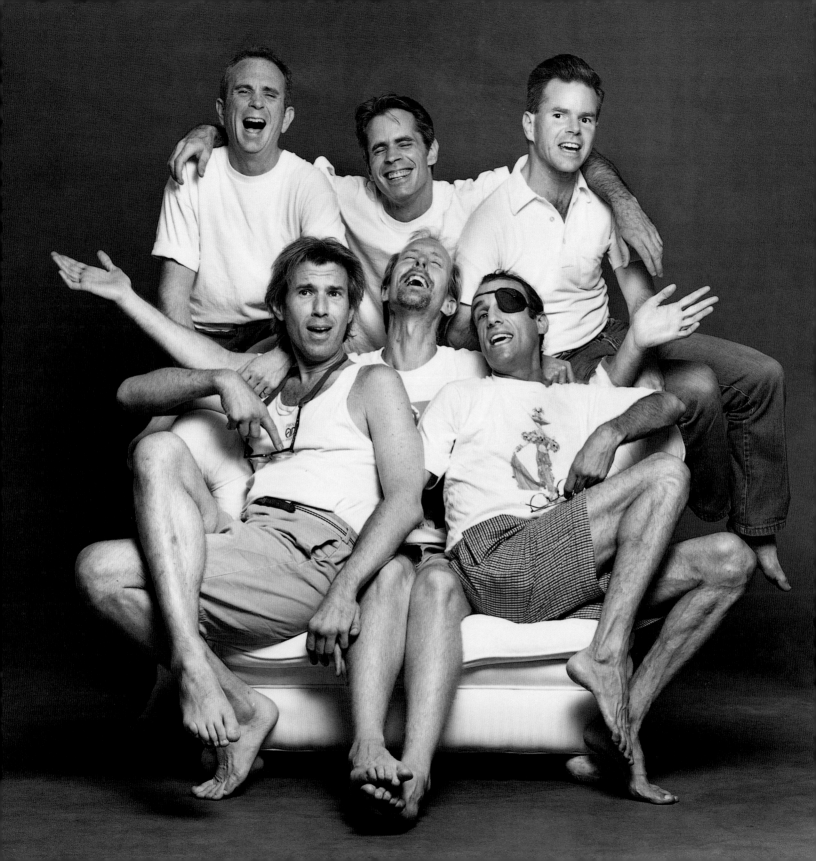

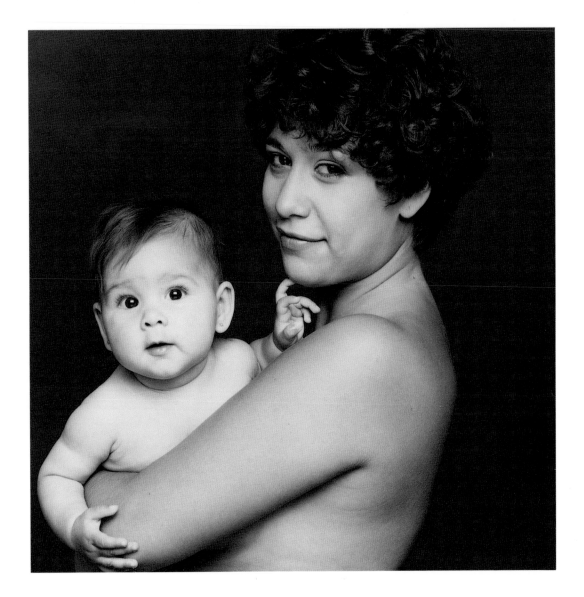

MARLENE DIAZ and her daughter

Margaretha keeps me going. I look at her and see the essence of life.

[OPPOSITE: CLOCKWISE FROM TOP LEFT]

**PHILLIP CROSS, MICHAEL GALT,
T. J. McSHERRY, MICHAEL MITCHELL,
DAVID HAGEN, and JEFFREY LACHOW
of Friends in Deed**

Photographed while performing their rendition of "Diamonds are a Girl's Best Friend."

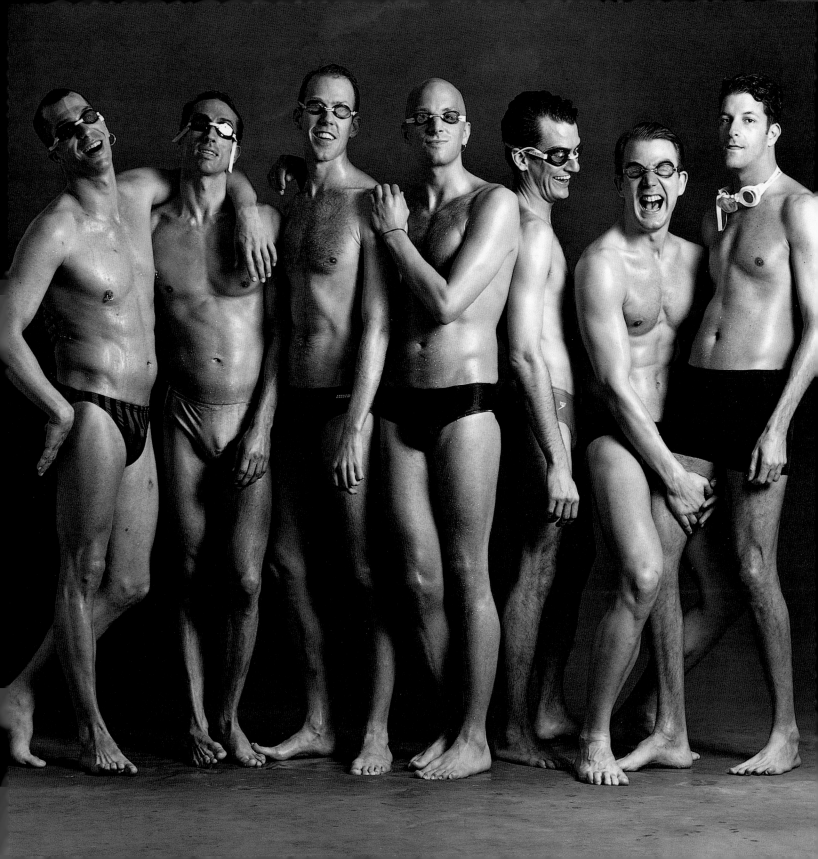

THE SWIM TEAM

Swimming provides a good excuse to shower with
thirty other guys.

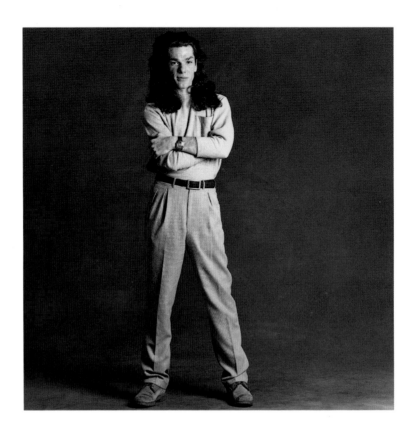

BREE SCOTT-HARTLAND
as Bree Scott-Hartland

They keep telling me I'm gonna die, so I have to live it up . . .

[OPPOSITE]

BREE SCOTT-HARTLAND
as Delphinia Blue

. . . and live up to it!

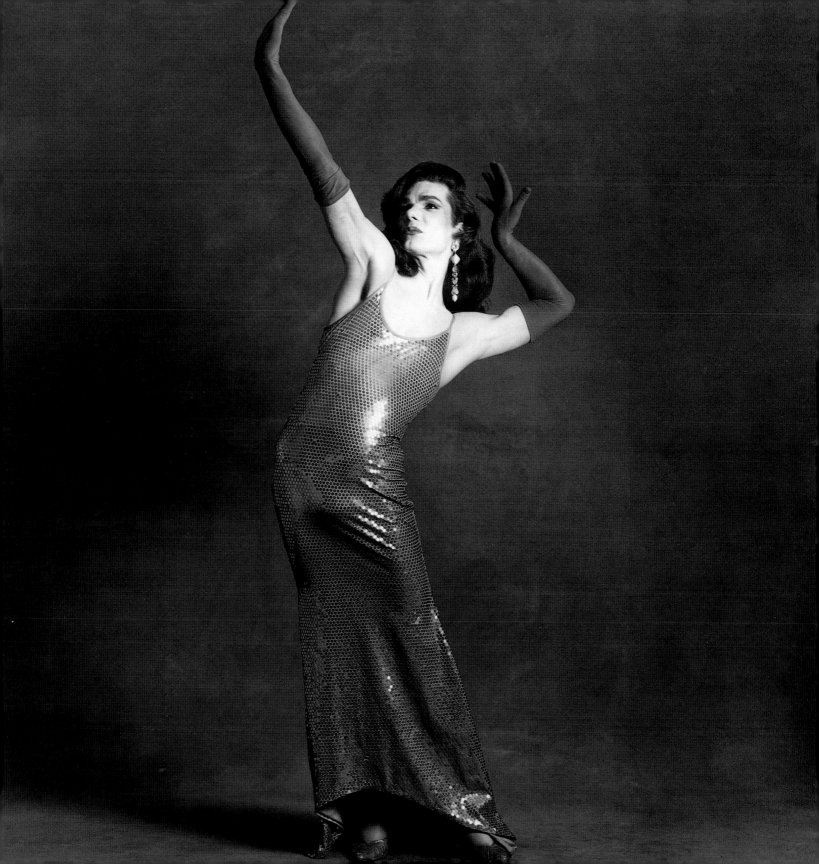

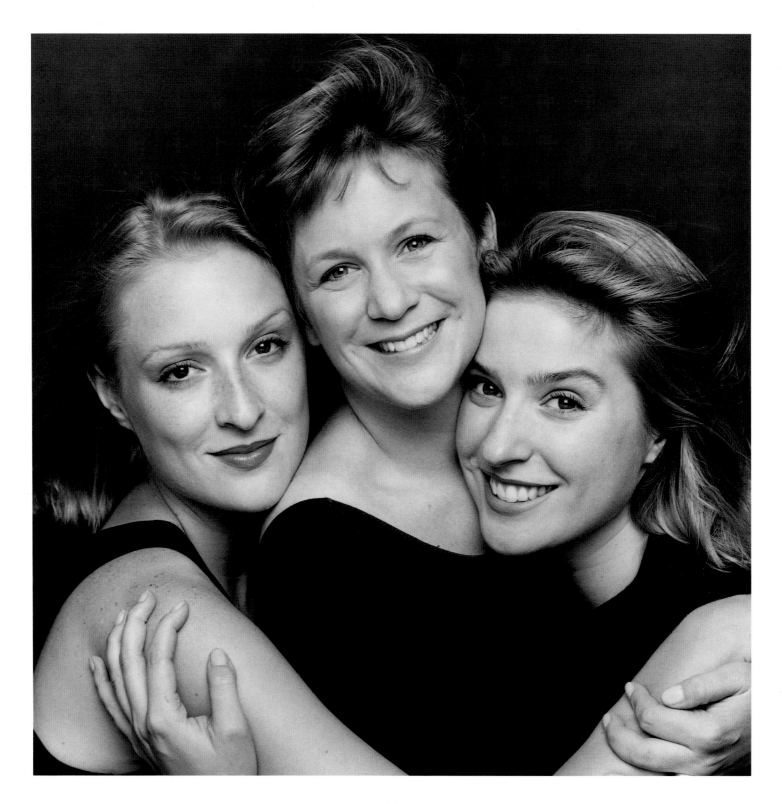

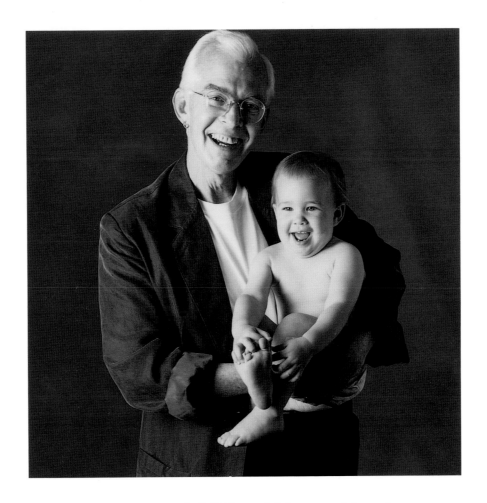

PHILLIP BROOKE and his granddaughter

AIDS has provided a constant reminder that today is all I have. I am truly blessed;
my wonderful daughter and son-in-law have never withheld my granddaughter
from me. Their love has been a source of great strength for me during hospital
stays and in healthier times. Love is all I'll take with me when I'm gone.

[OPPOSITE]

PAMELA SHAW (center) and her sisters

AIDS has been a mixed blessing for me; it has transformed my life in many
ways. In the two years since I found out that I carry the HIV virus, I have
learned more about myself than ever before. I also have more love in my life
than I ever thought possible. My positive diagnosis brought my family back
together at a time when we were beginning to grow apart. It's a good feeling
to know just how much my family and friends love and support me.

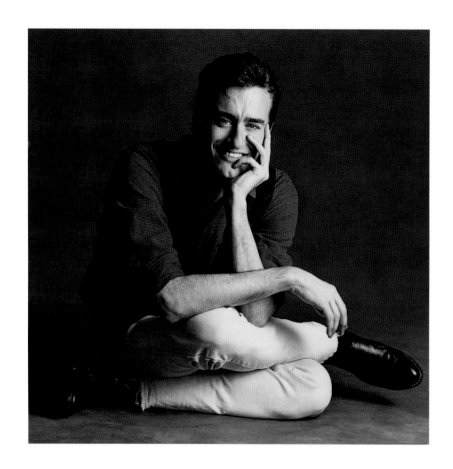

BRIAN REVIS

I took the HIV test three years ago because I wanted to father a child with a lesbian friend. I was shocked by the positive results, but I figured being stressed out didn't help matters. Eventually, it motivated me to do what I always wanted to do with my life, pursue a career in the theater. I was on my way to audition for *Oklahoma!* when I posed for Carolyn. I figured the costume would represent what I love the most: performing and expressing myself. I got the part.

[OPPOSITE]

STAN STOJ and Linda

Look at the people you're in contact with every day; some of them you confide in, some are very important to you. These people are not necessarily related by blood or by legal documents, but they are your family. Now imagine that all these people disappeared within a few years. This is the devastation caused by AIDS. Please realize that all people are important. And cherish those you love.

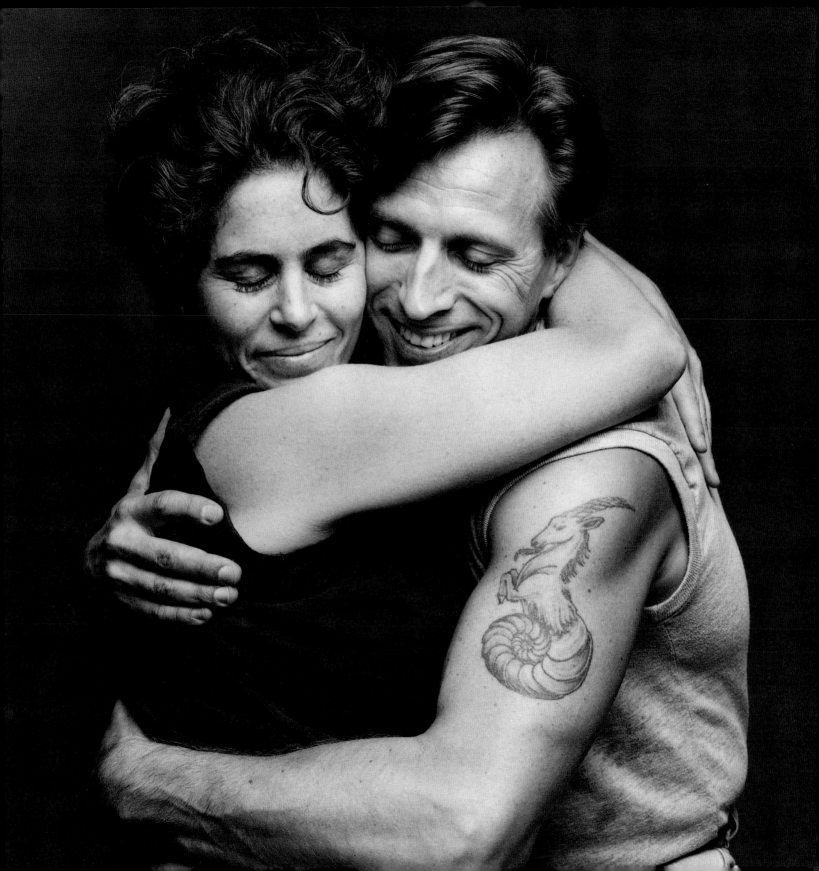

[OPPOSITE: CLOCKWISE FROM TOP LEFT]

PATRICK RIORDAN

When Carolyn asked me to bring something of meaning to the photo shoot, I couldn't think of anything, so I started going to therapy. I finally chose this "American Crochet" number— it started out as a poncho, but my friend Gene crocheted up the sides and made it into a mini. This image portrays my view of our chaotic world and its heavy veil of absurdity.

DENIS CORNELIUS

Do I look like a victim?

ROBERT POLENZ
(also known as Tomato Bob)

Bob sells tomatoes. If you call his machine you'll learn what vegetables are happening this week. Bob and his dog Bill have identical personalities—gentle and kind.

VINCE GABRIELLY

I do not waste time focusing on what is lost, but see the present and future as all-encompassing. What exists now is paramount.

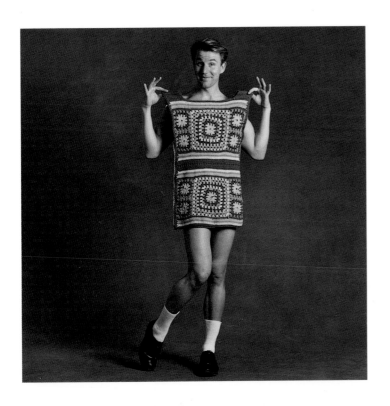

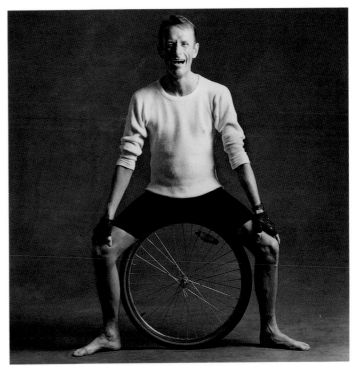

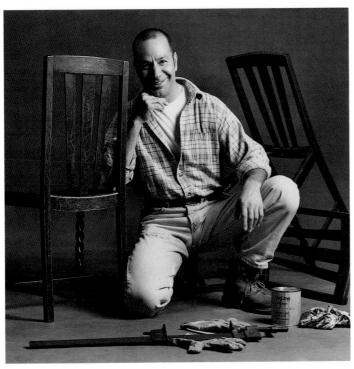

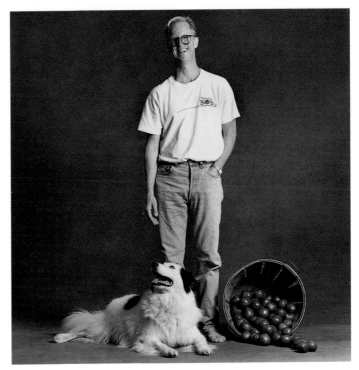

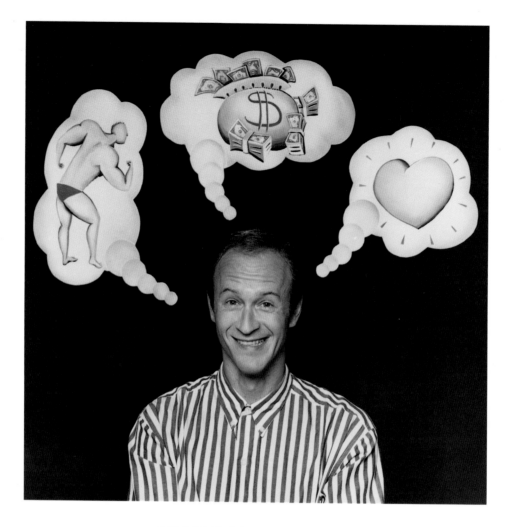

CHRISTOPHER NOBLE
creator of Nobleworks greeting cards
My dreams keep me happy and healthy.

[OPPOSITE: FROM LEFT TO RIGHT]
ALBERT TEN BRINK, age 47,
ARTHUR REHAK, age 41, **JOHN JONES,** age 45,
and **JOHN BASILE,** age 42
T-cells!

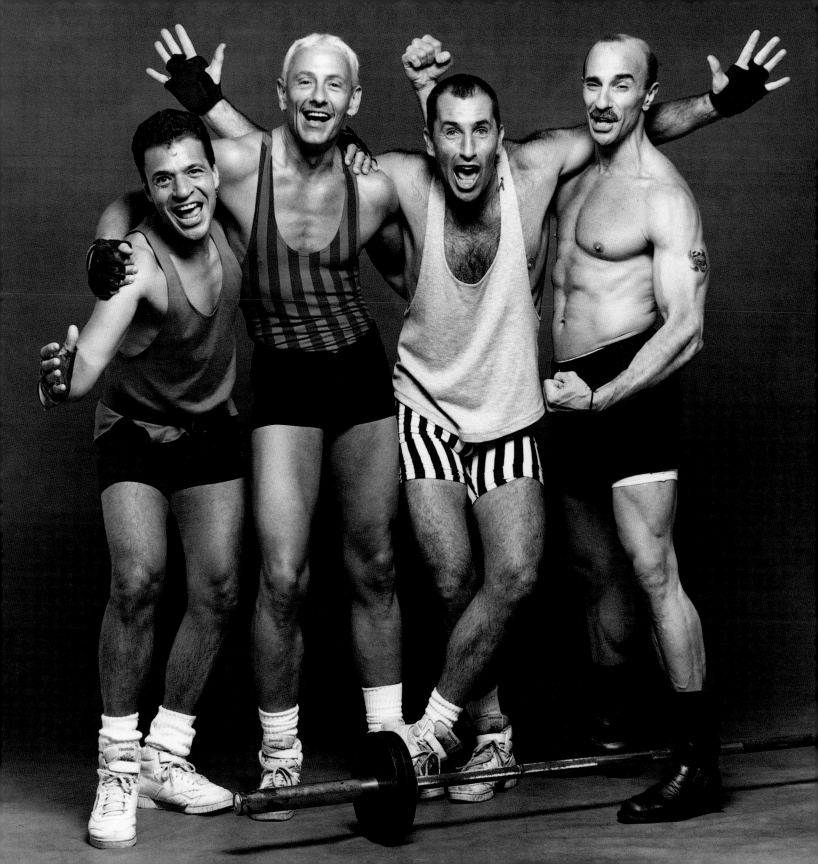

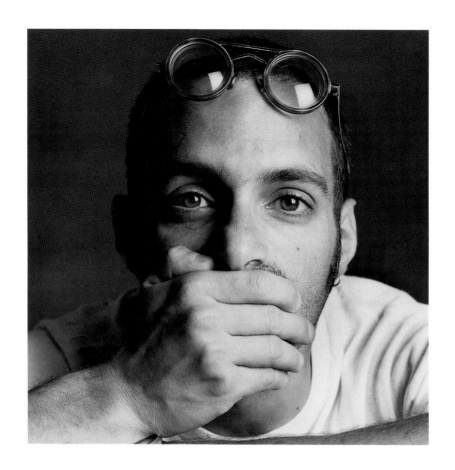

DAVID FEINBERG
author of *Spontaneous Combustion*

[O P P O S I T E]

RANDOLPH WINCHESTER KING, JR.

I was tested for HIV virtually as soon as the test was invented. Although I do not recall being alarmed or even very much surprised by the news that I tested positive, it was to change my life profoundly. Projects which were important to me became the all-consuming focus of my energy, as I then believed that I had between one thousand and ten thousand days to live. I applied to several Scottish universities to study Scots law. I recall commenting to my Washington psychiatrist that a university is a good place to die; like a shot he fired back, "A university is a great place to live." On December 5, 1992, the University of Glasgow awarded me my fourth university degree, a Bachelor of Laws in Scots law. Still believing that my physical body is allotted to me for between one thousand and ten thousand more days, I now plan to circumnavigate the world under sail.

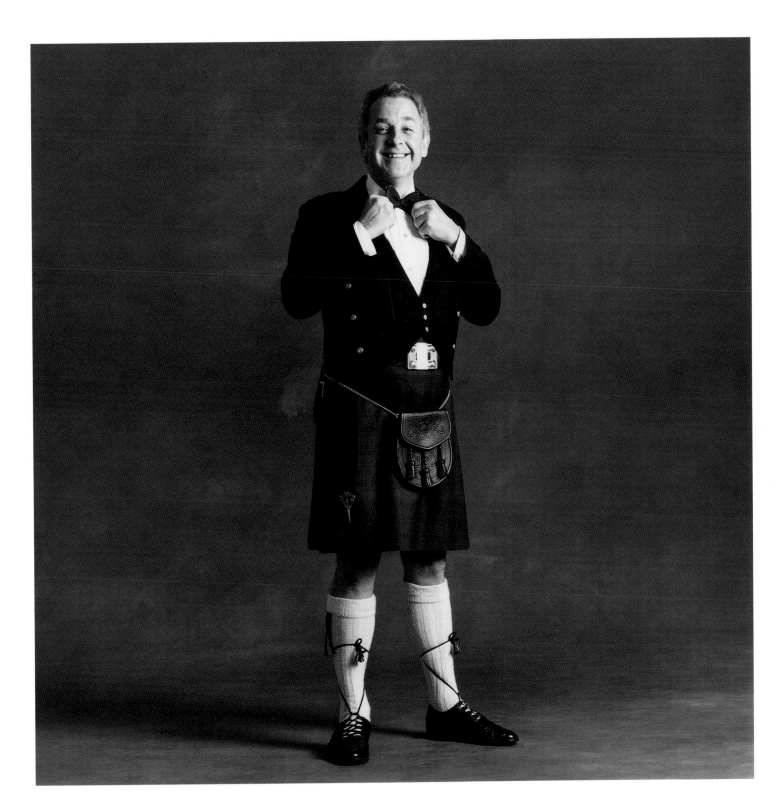

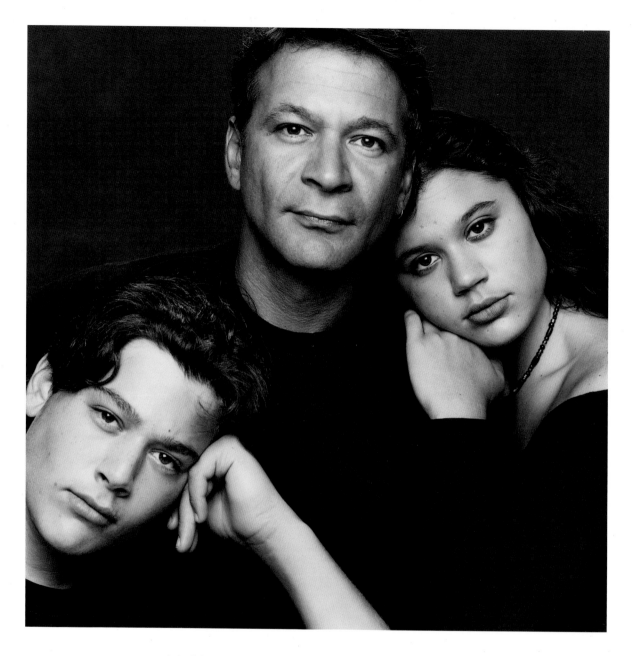

JACK ROSENBERG and his children

If there is one thing I'm sure of, it's that this disease may change your life, but it doesn't end it.
It becomes a part of you, just one part. It doesn't define you, and it definitely doesn't destroy you.
Have I learned to live with it? Yes, I have. Would I trade it away? In a second.

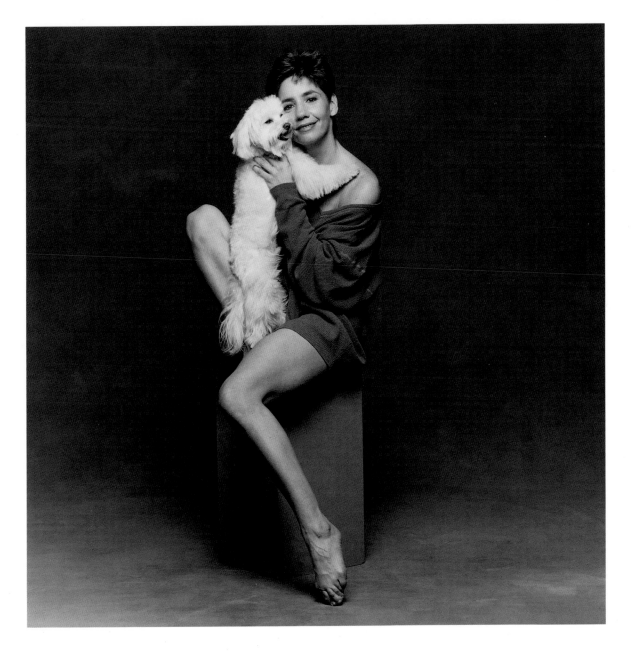

ROBIN HOROWITZ

I was always afraid of something—death, other people. There was no room in my life for living.
I joined Alcoholics Anonymous and cleaned myself up, but I slipped right back when I found out I
was HIV positive. The virus preyed on all of my worst fears, and I fell further and further down
until I realized that maybe my fears were based on self-centeredness. Maybe my real reason to be
here was to help other people. I wouldn't want my life without the lessons I've learned from AIDS.

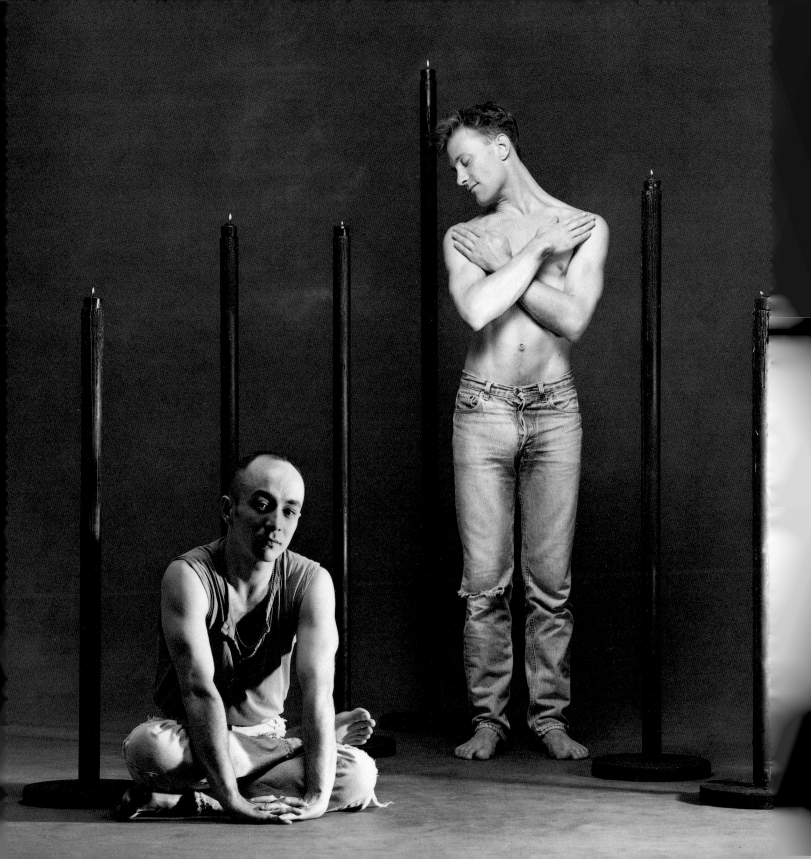

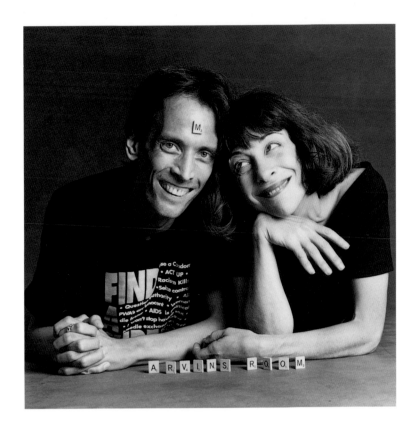

SCOTT McPHERSON (1959–1992)
author of *Marvin's Room,*
and Laura Esterman, actress

Scott created a wondrous play, *Marvin's Room,* and a beautiful character, Bessie, out of his own soul, and gave them to the world. He was able to live his life fully, gently, and with humor, even in the face of his own mortality. He had a deliciously tart side as well. To quote Bessie's words: "I'm so lucky to have been able to love somebody so much. I'm so lucky to have loved so much. I'm so lucky."

[OPPOSITE]
CHUCK BROWN
director of *The Night Larry Kramer Kissed Me* (left),
and David Drake, actor and playwright

I'm not afraid to think about dying, but I'm not leaving before I've told my stories. My stories, and the stories of my gay family, are our truths. My work brings me closer to a sense of justice.

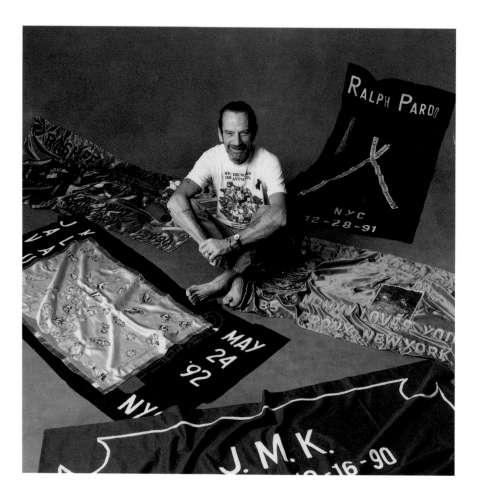

BOB WILSON
Director of the Metro New York Quilters

I've been HIV positive since 1985, and my doctor tells me that quilting is what keeps me going. I had never actually sewn a quilt before this spring, when I began working on the AIDS memorial quilt. I just looked at the enormous pile of work to be done and said to myself, this can't be that hard. Of course, I had to rip my first quilt apart about thirty times. The quilt is such a powerful statement, yet so sad. I once heard a woman say it was the most beautiful cemetery she had ever seen.

[OPPOSITE]
PATRICK J. O'CONNELL
Director, Visual AIDS (creators of the Ribbon Project and organizers of Day Without Art and Night Without Light)

Everyone is living with AIDS, some of us are just more aware of it than others. Though the pandemic continues to rage, there is still no cure. The best we have is education and education begins with dialogue. So, daily, I'll continue to greet each opportunity with a smile, to wear my red ribbon, and to never stop talking.

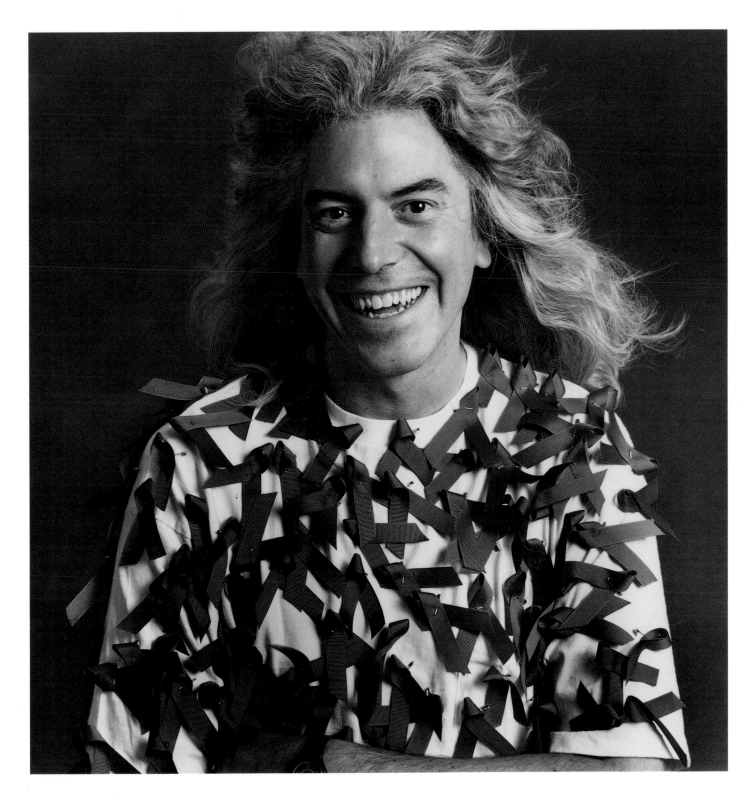

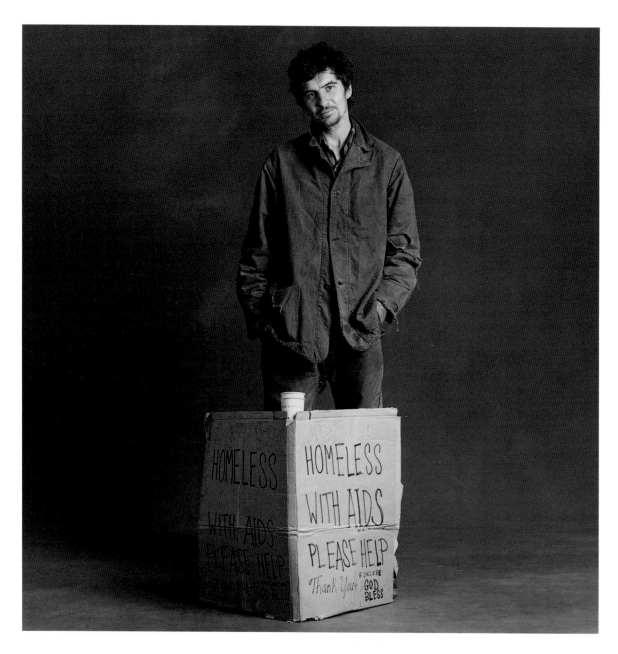

JOE O'HARA

Joe is homeless by choice.

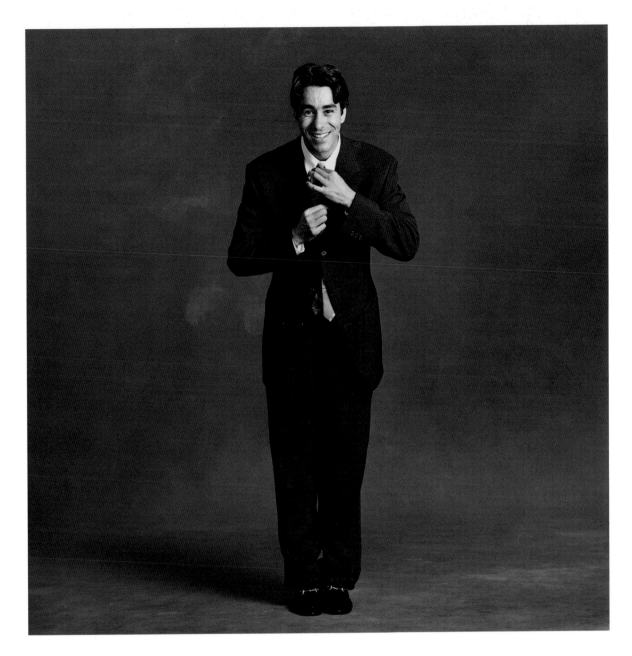

BARRY MIGUEL

I'm the same person that I was five years ago; I feel exactly the same. But in fact, I'm sick—or at least I have a compromised immune system. And that's very hard to accept. How should I relate to society, and how should society relate to me? Being HIV positive is like living in a world unto itself, like belonging to a clique of sorts. Today I have a new circle of friends, a new education, and a new vocabulary. All of this definitely comes under the heading of things you never wanted to know, but do.

PHILLIP GILMORE, actor/singer;
TOM VIOLA, managing director, Broadway Cares/
Equity Fights AIDS;
DICK GALLAGHER, composer/musical director, *Front*;
HENRY MENENDEZ, actor/singer;
LEE RAINES, actor/dancer; **PATRICK KERR**, actor;
DENNIS CROWLEY, press agent

The theater community has rallied to raise funds and offer assistance to people with AIDS and AIDS service organizations as few other industries have. Still, there is a deep fear within the industry that one's HIV-positive status will be revealed before one actually appears sick. Many think to themselves: "Who will hire me now? Will I ever work again?" There are more of us than you know, working every day, doing eight performances a week, month after month, in a variety of jobs, for years. Being "out" is ultimately the only way we can move past this unspoken fear. Hopefully this photograph will stir personal and professional examination of this dilemma. Perhaps a few more will step forward or, at least, allow others not to fear disclosure, if only among their friends and colleagues. We are not poster boys. We are working professionals. Many of you applaud the work we do. And, like so many others you are unaware of, we are all HIV positive.

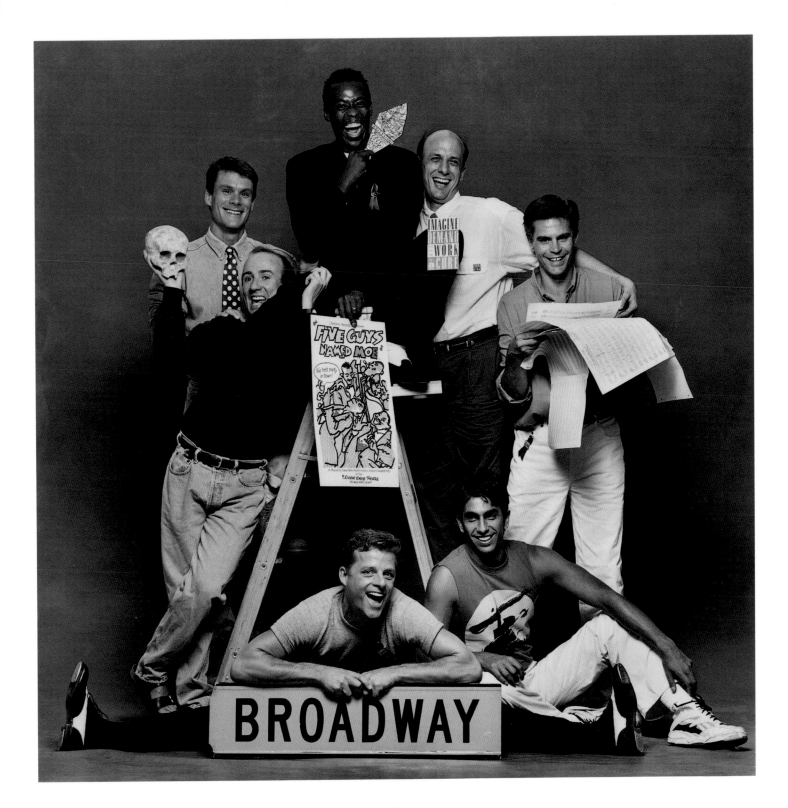

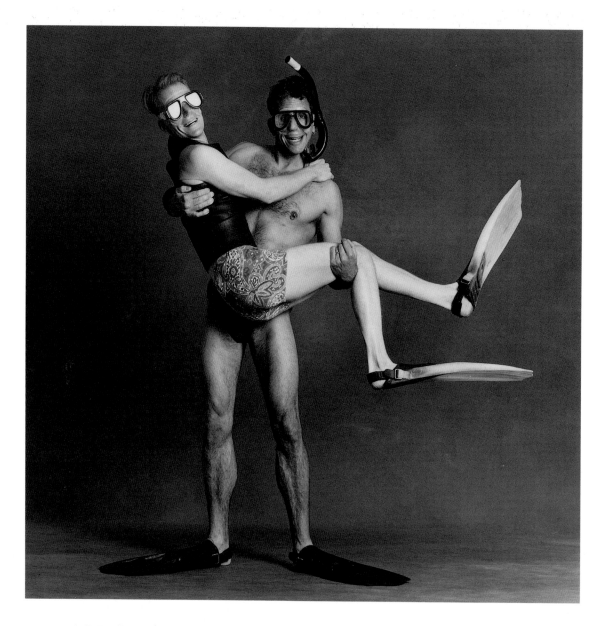

LEE CHASTAIN and MICHAEL SHERNOFF (standing)
My life was incomplete till Shern swept me off my feet.

[OPPOSITE]
**LOUIS ARCE's children (from left to right):
JOEL, ANGEL, and Noel**
I don't think I would be alive if it weren't for them.

70

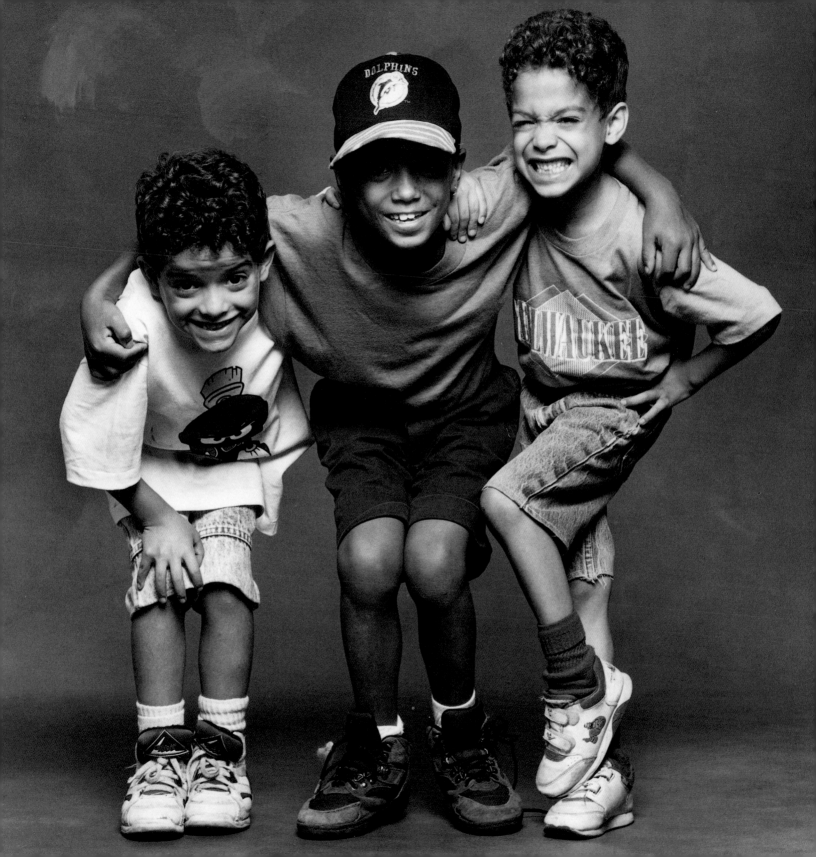

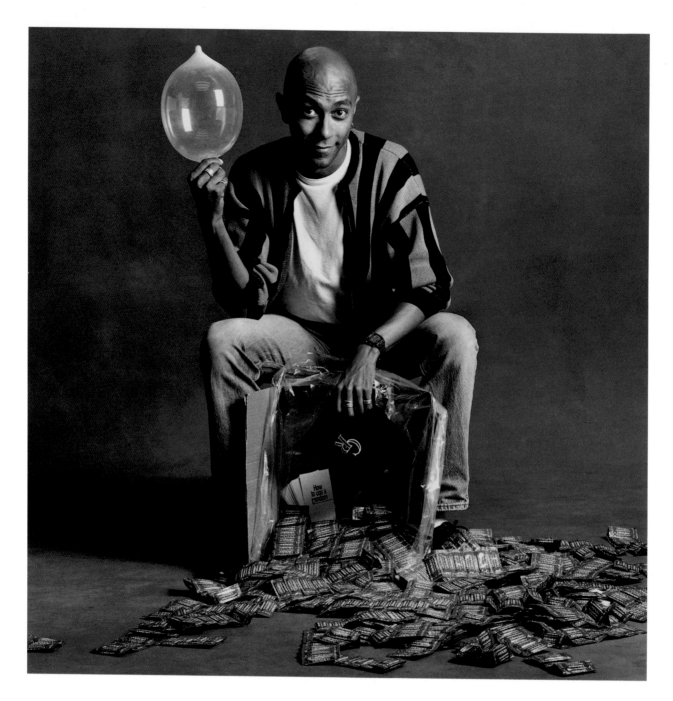

ROBERT VASQUEZ
AIDS activist

It's about safer sex and condoms. It's about education and information. It's about treating ourselves and each other with respect, responsibility, and love. It's about life.

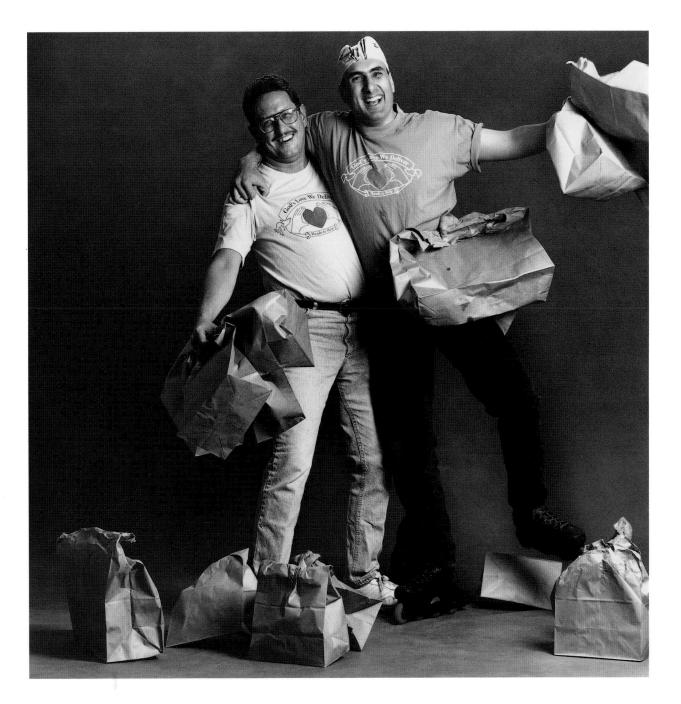

JIM KONETSKY (left) and JAMES SCUTERO
of God's Love We Deliver
God's Love We Deliver provides hot meals for homebound people with AIDS.

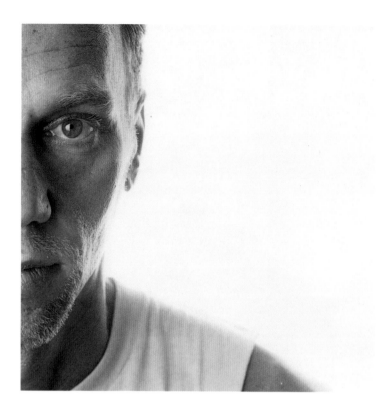

STEVEN LIPOSKI

My AIDS diagnosis got me in gear to change my life. While shoveling out from under the pile of garbage
I had dumped on myself, I discovered the light within us all. Sisters and Brothers, we are love, and love heals.

[OPPOSITE]

INMATES FROM S.T.E.P. (Self-Taught Empowerment and Pride Program)
at Rikers Island Correctional Facility

Why do we hold these hands?
We hold these hands because we care!

"God grant me the serenity
to accept the things I cannot change,
the courage to change the things I can,
and the wisdom to know the difference."

[Reinhold Niebuhr]

It works if you work it!
I am somebody!
I am somebody!

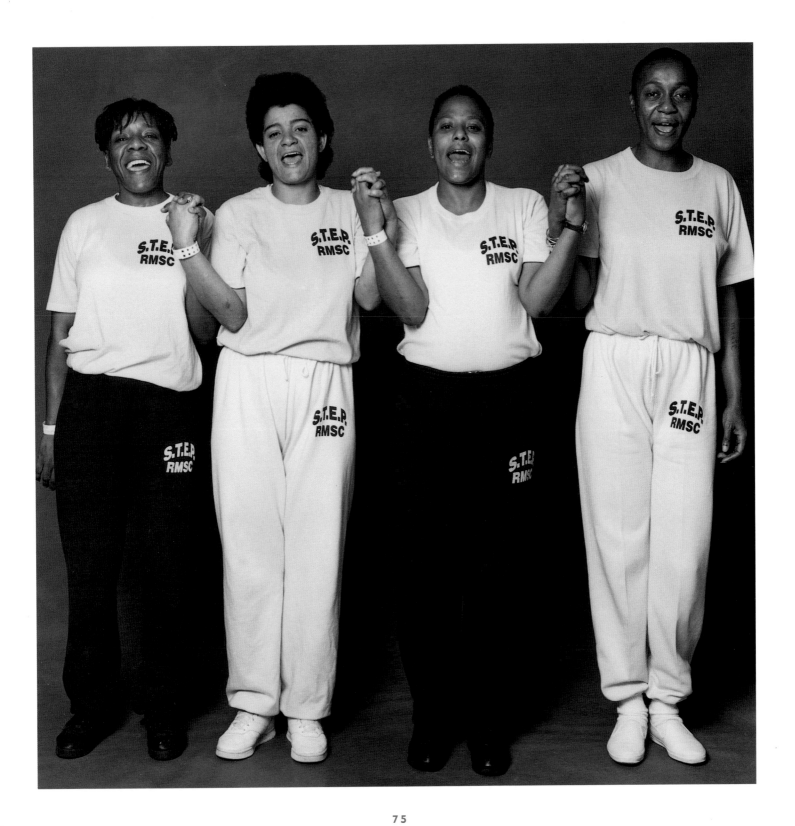

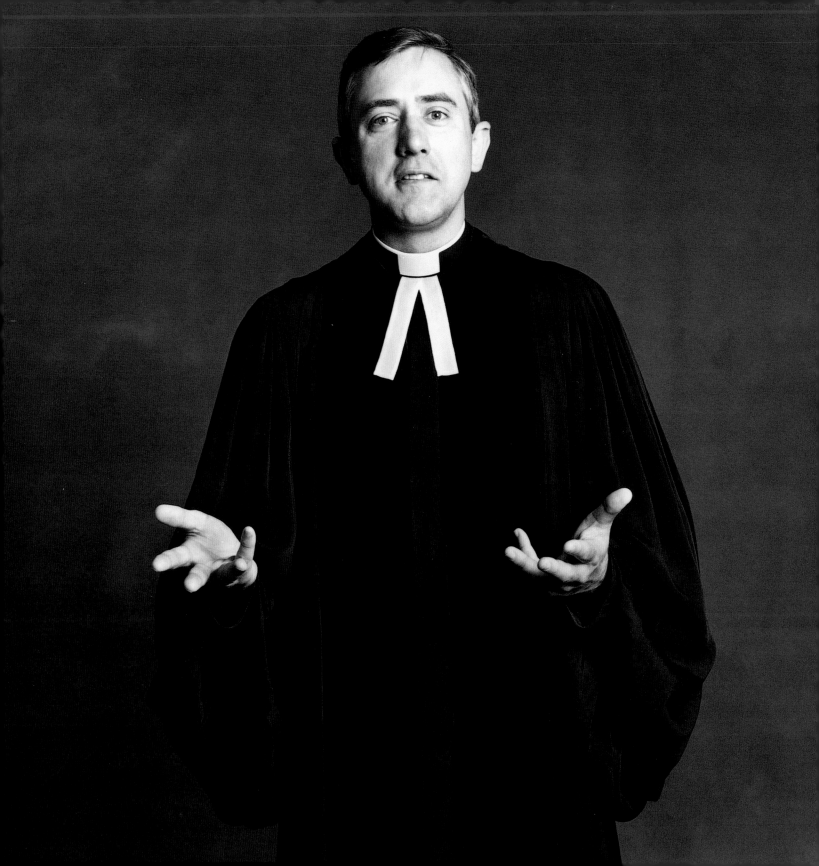

THE REVEREND STUART D. SMITH
Presbyterian Pastor

Religious ministry at its best offers not comfort or guidance, but power and vision. When I wear my clerical collar into one of the gay bars in my parish, when I joke with the bartender, or hang out on the streets with young men engaging in prostitution, I demonstrate that you don't need to be dressed up and sitting respectfully in a stained glass fortress to be part of the community of faith. I'm the pastor for those who don't feel welcome in church. Most of my parish is the streets and bars of the gay community of Chicago. My HIV status matters little to my parishioners. They want someone to listen to their stories and help them make sense of their lives. If my positive status means anything to my parishioners, it means that even in sickness, we are not alone.

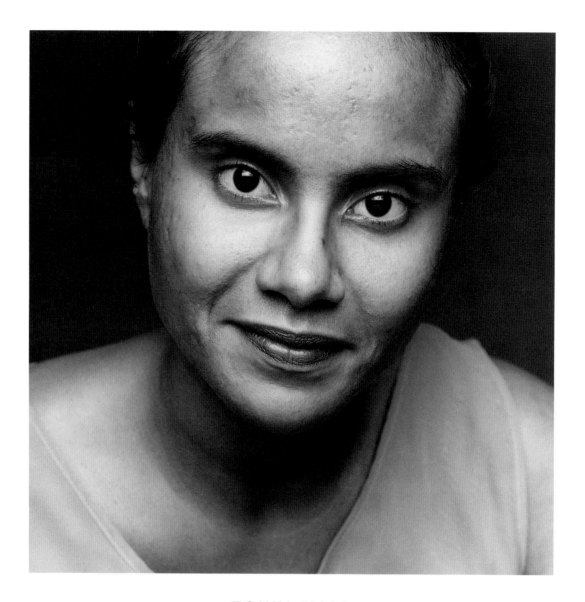

TONYA HALL

I have lost sixty-nine friends since December 26, 1991. That's when I started counting.
I remember that day because it was the day after Christmas and I had two funerals to go to.
They were both for people under thirty years old.

[OPPOSITE]

KEVIN SHORE (center) and friends

I feel so lucky to be a part of this project. This photo hangs in my living room, and whenever
someone sees it, a conversation about life, love, and AIDS always begins.

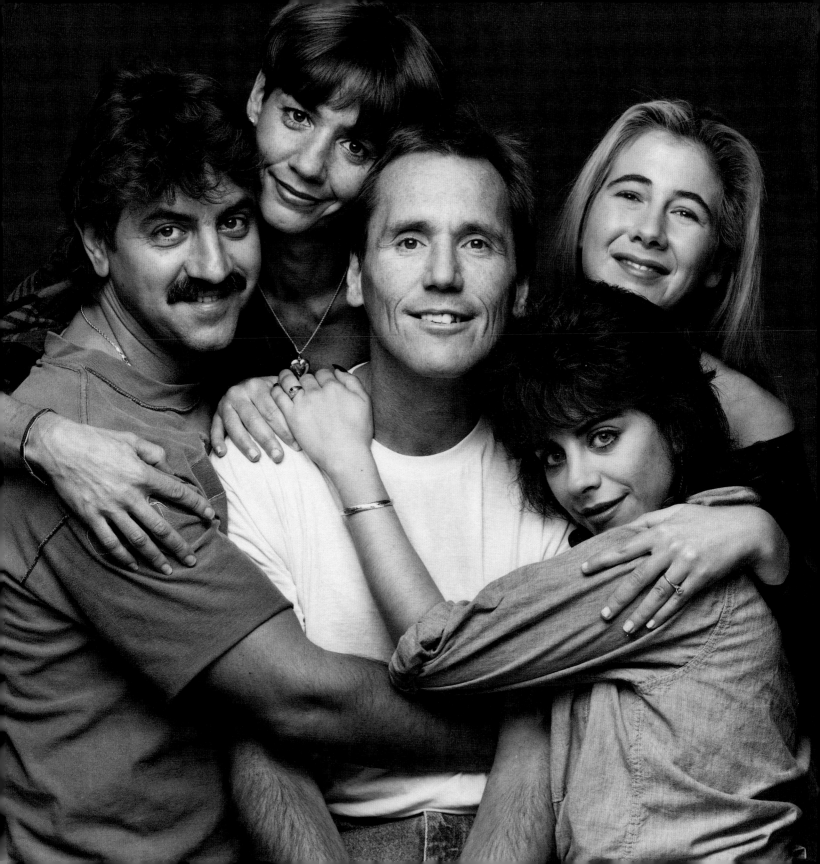

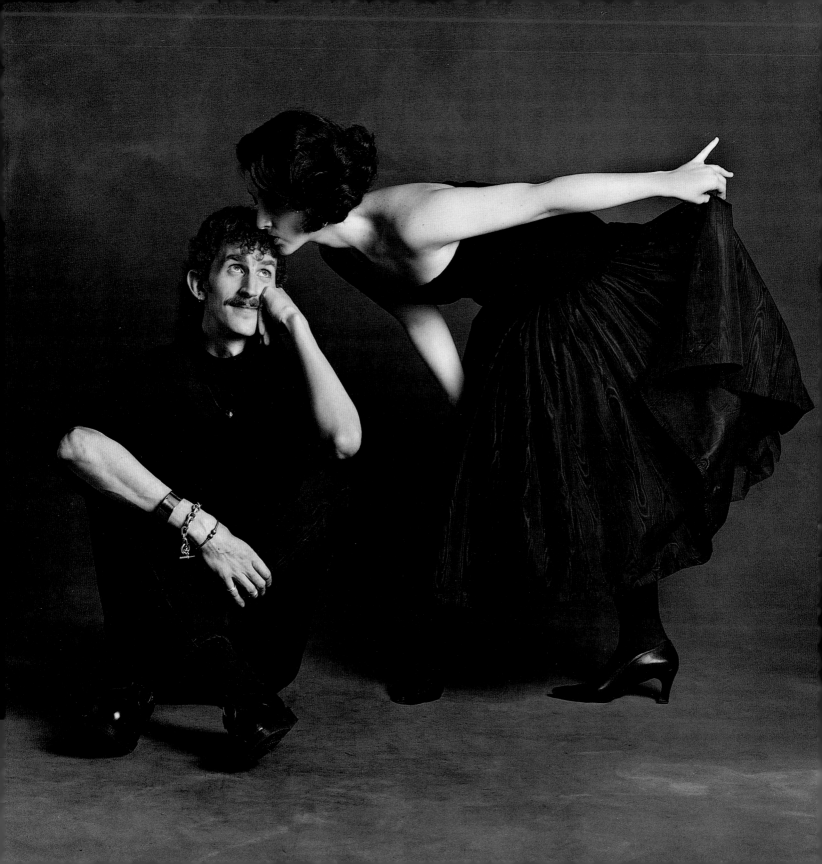

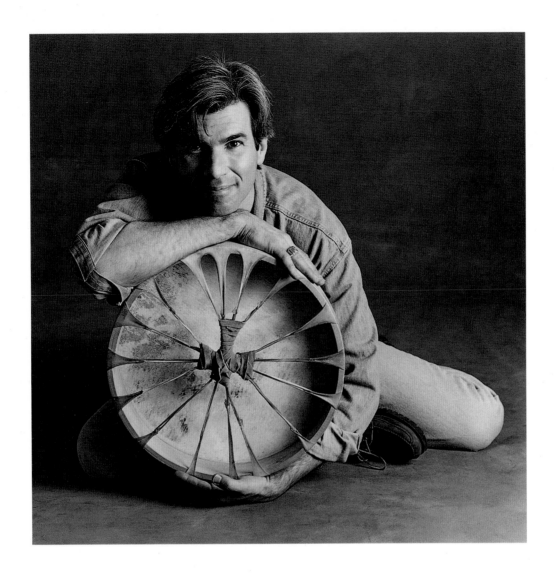

JEFFREY LACHOW
Heartbeat: the rhythm of life, life, life.

[OPPOSITE]
GORDON ROGERS and Victoria
Victoria is my best friend, and has always been there for me when I needed her.
Everyone needs a Victoria in their life—most people have one, they just aren't aware
of it. I made this dress for her because she's a real party girl, and a real party girl
needs a real party dress.

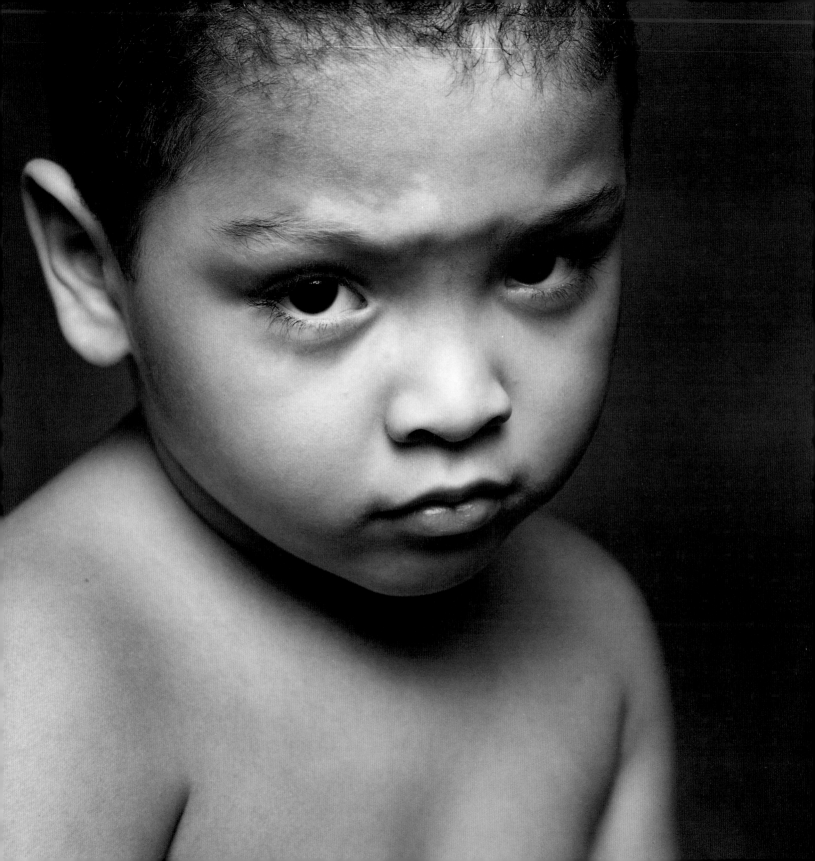

ISAAC CHABRIER, age 3

Isaac tested positive for the virus at birth, but his status has since
converted to HIV negative.

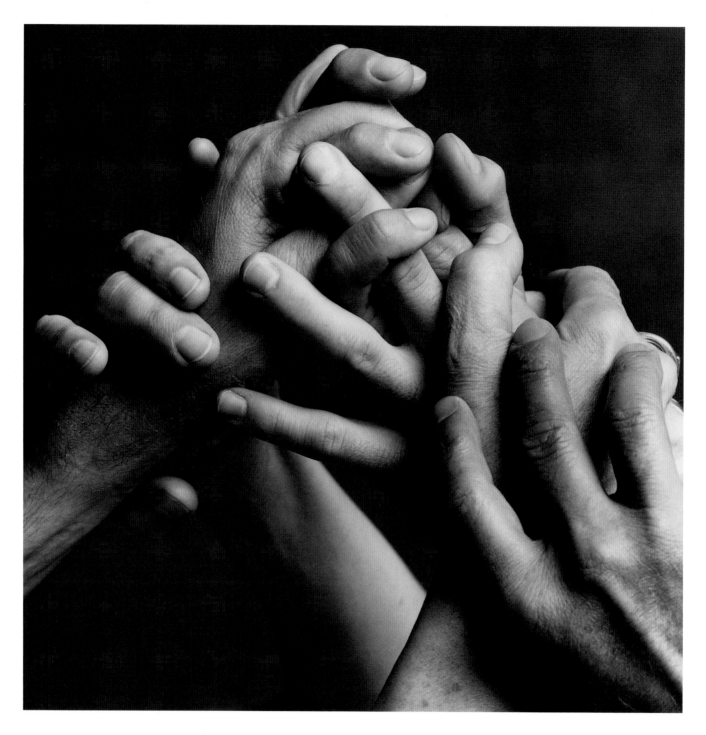

Friends in Deed is dedicated to providing emotional, spiritual, and psychological support
to all those confronting a life-threatening illness.

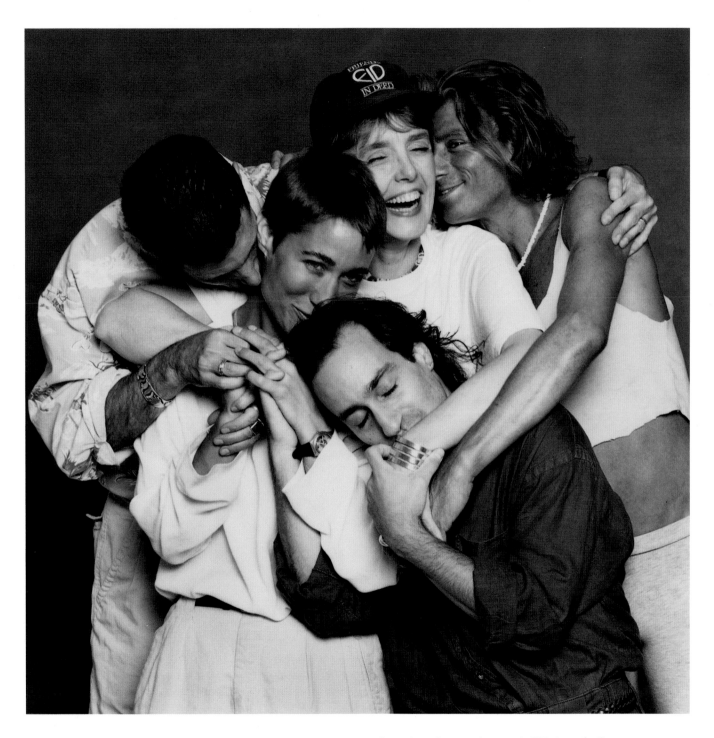

Friends in Deed: Cy O'Neal, founder (with cap), and "Friends"

I would like to thank the following people who had the courage and
took the time to come to my studio with people and things that they love.
Unfortunately, not everyone I photographed could appear in the book;
but I am forever grateful to you for allowing me a glimpse of your life:

RICK AISHMAN

HENRY BAKER

MIKE BARR

JOHN BERRIOS

SUSAN BROWN

LUIS LOPEZ DETRES

CATHERINE DONARUMO

THOMAS DUANE

DONNA GARRAFFA

MICHAEL LINKS

BAMBI MAGIE

DAVID MANDEL

DAVE McMINN

STEVE METZGER

CHERYL MILLS

ILEANA RIVERA

DENNIS ROMAN

PETER STALEY

MICHAEL PAUL WASKO

JASON WORTH

AFTERWORD

While working on *Living Proof* I was often asked how I felt about meeting the people who participated in this project. This experience has brought me much sorrow and much joy. It is always sad to lose someone you've met, and yet I wouldn't trade one day of working on this book for anything. In the last two years, I have learned more about human beings than I ever would have imagined. From my first meeting with a participant, I was amazed at how open and forthcoming people were. Most of the subjects responded to a flyer that basically said, "If you are living positively with HIV/AIDS, call me." These individuals had already come to a certain stage of understanding their illness—in most cases they had come to terms with it and accepted it. These people had no façades; they opened their hearts and souls to me readily, giving me an opportunity to find out how people really react in the face of great adversity. And you know what? People truly are extraordinary. While taking these photographs, I kept thinking of a line I once heard: "As human beings we are at our best when things are at their worst." The people I was meeting exemplified this.

I cannot close my eyes to the injustices that I have witnessed surrounding this disease, nor to the stories that I have heard about the stigma attached to it, nor to the hurt inflicted by ignorance and prejudice. But I have learned that just when you might think there isn't any hope, well, there *is*. I have seen racial and sexual barriers break down and people come together for one another. I have witnessed unbelievable support for others—people caring, giving, and helping when others are in need. I have seen those who have the least to give, give up the little they have in order to help someone else. It has been a great honor to meet these people; each and every one of them has taught me something that I will never forget.

A project like this could never have been done alone, and I am so grateful to all those who came through for me. I can't possibly thank everyone, yet there are a few people I would like to mention here. Georgia Goodrow, who works with me, was instrumental to the completion of this project. She accepted each new challenge no matter how much work it required, and I am eternally grateful for her dedication. Michael Liberatore has a gift with words that continues to amaze me; I cannot imagine anyone else working on the text of this book as well and as thoughtfully as he did. Michael is one of the kindest, most compassionate men I have ever known; every time I asked him for more help he was there, ready and willing. Will Guilliams had a vision for this project from the very beginning, and he sat in his office many late evenings working tirelessly. I also want to thank my husband, Jacques Borris, whose love and support made it possible for me to complete *Living Proof* in a spirit of deep gratitude and inspiration. And to George DeSipio, who originally thought of the idea for *Living Proof*—I hope that I have helped realize your dream, George. A sincere thank-you to my editor, Laura Straus, for understanding this project, believing in it, and never losing sight of what our direction should be. And to everyone at Abbeville—thank you for taking a chance with this book. I think we can open some eyes and provide a ray of hope.

—**CAROLYN JONES,** New York City, 1993

ACKNOWLEDGMENTS

Francis Catania

Melissa Syd Chimovitz

The Cowles Charitable Trust

Design Industries Foundation for AIDS

Duggal Color Projects, Inc.

Eastman Kodak Company

Rose Frisenda

Hiro

Simon Horobin

New York Foundation for the Arts

Polaroid Corporation

Hans Peter Weiss

Carl Asakawa

Bryan Baldwin

Andrea Benco

John Bennette

Nina Chernik

Cleary, Gottlieb, Steen & Hamilton

Kermit Cole

Common Boundary

Daffy's

Debevoise & Plimpton

George DeSipio, Sr.

Beth Rudin Dewoody

Jenny Dixon

Bob Fennell

Philip Galanes

Adam J. Goodman

Thaddeus Grimes-Gruczka

A. H. Haynes & Co.

Howard M. Jenkins

Chris Kovarik

Rosemary Kuropat

Martino & Co.

Motel Fine Arts

Out Magazine

Parish-Hadley Associates

Petrik Frames

Susan Romano

Seventeen Magazine

Charles Simon

Susan Swimmer

Marina Urbach

Bob Valenti

Victor Hasselblad Inc.

Tom Viola

Todd Watts

Brock Wylan